← Basil

Printed and bound by Butler Tanner & Dennis, Frome, Somerset.

First published in 2013 by Fox School Association, Kensington Place, London W8 7PP. Reg. Charity No. 1087097.

Text © 2013 Fox School Association.

This book is dedicated to the children, staff, families and friends of Fox Primary School whose delight in sitting down together, at tables laden with food they want to share, inspired our devotion to this book.

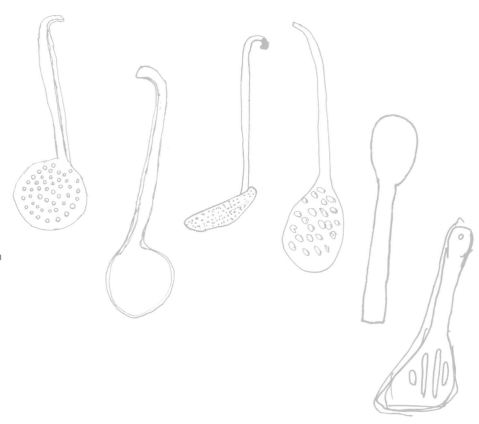

FOX

from the kitchens of notting hill

POT

CONTENTS

FOREWARD

Fox is a vibrant community school in the heart of Notting Hill. Our school community is comprised of over 40 different nationalities, and incorporates a rich spectrum of languages and cultures.

Our parents and carers are deeply invested in the school and this is nowhere more evident than at our annual International Evening – a celebration of diverse cultures, which showcases food and drink from around the world. The support and response from the Fox parents and carers to the International Evening has been overwhelming, and gave rise to the idea of a recipe book drawn from contributions from the Fox community.

I feel that this book is the perfect synthesis of what we here at Fox are trying to achieve. We have free-range chickens, a beehive producing fantastic honey and a bountiful allotment garden. The children are a part of this fruitful ecology, and it is brought into their learning at school. Additionally, we have a long-term commitment to healthy food, reflected in the meals created on-site by our professional chef, Nina.

This recipe book will stand as a celebration of our rich make-up, of the dedication of our wider community and will raise money for our school as well as those charities we support.

Enjoy!

Paul Cotter
Head Teacher
Fox Primary School

INTRODUCTION

Home cooking is alive and well and likely to remain so – which would come as no surprise to contributors to the fabulous Fox Pot, a collection of recipes for the kind of cooking you won't find anywhere else but in the home – if not yours, then someone else's.

Home cooks, whenever they set up house elsewhere, bring their traditions with them, adapting to new ingredients but staying true to the way they like to cook – maybe not every day, but certainly at family gatherings or when extending hospitality to friends. And it's this, the practical expression of a wish to share who we are through the good things we set on the table, which transforms a community of strangers into friends.

Fox Primary School is a remarkable institution in many ways, not least in the recognition that families do matter, and that who they are and what they do is worthy of celebration. Diversity – and these pages are ample proof of how different we all are – is valued as a strength, a way of uniting, and this is at no time more evident than when the school opens its gates and celebrates diversity at the fairs and entertainments which take place throughout the year.

As a cookery writer, with a particular interest in home-cooking, I have long been an enthusiastic sampler of the dishes on offer at those Fox gatherings to which parents (and teachers) contribute refreshments. Such events are always lively and well-attended and offer a chance for the wider community to get together and share a common interest. And it has always seemed to me – never mind that the stalls raise much-needed money for the school – that the most important element of the whole event, quite apart from the astonishing diversity of cuisines and high level of culinary skill, is the pride taken in good food and pleasure in the chance to share it with others. Since national flags adorn the stalls and everyone is always keen to sample everyone else's cooking and discuss the recipes, it's these enquiries which became the seedcorn for this book.

Many of us still like to cook, in spite of all that's said and written otherwise, particularly those with families. Home cooks will always find a way to make everyday ingredients taste good in the time it takes to get food on the table, which is what this book is all about. On a practical level, contributions have been edited for clarity alone, allowing the authors' voices to be heard. To keep the arrangement simple, the recipes are divided into courses – starters, mains, sides and desserts – which takes us from Hannah Pernerup's classic Swedish Gravad Lax with mustard sauce to Kezia Pierce's Hot Spiced Cider. The photographs are of the dishes exactly as cooked to contributors' recipes, so that you can expect the same appetising results in your own kitchen.

You'll find plenty of authentic regional recipes many of which have been adapted to ingredients available in the UK. Among these are Joy Wu's elegant Chinese Vegetarian Steamed Buns (a winner at Fox's International Evenings); Irina Kazanchuk's modernised version of the traditional Ukrainian Borscht; Hazel Seow's Prawn Toasts (everyone's favourite Chinese finger food); the Hanh family's child-friendly Vietnamese Spring Rolls (the stuffing is what we all need to know); Elsa Pereira's finger-licking Mozambique Spiced Tiger Prawns – and that's just a few of the starters.

Not everything fits neatly into its allotted grouping – isn't that always the way when cooking for family and friends? – which means that robust main course candidates such as Turkish Tarhana soup feature in the Starters section and Bara Brith, Wales's fruity tea-bread, is tucked into the Desserts section along with the secrets of Will Sarne's Chocolate, Banana and Avocado Shake, while store cupboard specials such as Barbara Bird's Runner Bean Chutney (lovely with strong cheddar) and Fox School cook Nina Rich's Spiced Tomato Chutney are shelved in Sides.

In other words, with over eighty scrumptious recipes to explore and good friends to guide you along the way, there's something here for everyone, experienced or novice. But most particularly for those (big or small) who don't yet know (but are keen to find out) that what happens in the kitchen is the most fun a person can have with a sharp knife, a sturdy cooking pot, reliable heat source and a little help from a friend – which, as you'll see from the pages of this book, is pretty much all it takes.

Elisabeth Luard
Food writer, journalist, Fox granny

starters

gravad lax

Fresh and sweet and gently flavoured, this recipe is springtime itself. Hannah's children absolutely love it and would eat it all year round, however it's traditionally prepared for Easter, on Good Friday. It has a lovely soft sweetness that children really enjoy, but if you have some left over it is also delicious with some brown bread and a salad.

1	kilogram fresh salmon
4	tablespoons caster sugar
4	tablespoons salt
1	tablespoon white peppercorn
100	grams dill, chopped

FOR THE MUSTARD AND DILL SAUCE (HOVMÄSTARSÅS)

2	tablespoons mild, sweet mustard
1	teaspoon Dijon mustard
2	tablespoons sugar
1½	tablespoons white wine vinegar
200	millilitres sunflower oil
	Chopped dill
	Salt and white pepper

1 Cut the salmon into two equal fillet pieces. Keep the skin on.

2 Crush the white pepper and mix it with sugar, salt and dill. Rub half of the blend on the flesh side of each salmon fillet.

3 Spread the remainder of the salt-mixture on one of the fillets and fit the other on top of it, skin side up, to make a sandwich.

4 Rotate it so the thick edge of one fillet fits on top of the thin edge of the other and then put the fillets in a plastic bag and seal it well.

5 Keep it in the refrigerator for 48 hours and turn the bag a couple of times.

6 After two days, unwrap the cured fish, pat it dry and scrape off most of the cure and chopped dill. Slice the fish into thin pieces and serve with boiled potatoes and mustard and dill sauce.

THE SAUCE

1 Mix all the ingredients to a smooth sauce.

SERVES 8 AS A STARTER

cracked wheat salad

Sally Clarke is the owner and chef at renowned Notting Hill restaurant and bakery, Clarke's, on Kensington Church Street. Sally says about her salad, "I have never understood why every cracked wheat salad recipe I have ever read calls for first soaking the wheat in water. But what is more tasteless than water? Instead, at the restaurant, I make a pungent, spicy and flavourful juice out of the skins and seeds of the tomatoes. I believe that this is what makes our cracked wheat salad the best. It improves – if that is possible – on keeping a day or so." We've tested this salad and it's true to say it packs a real punch!

650 grams firm but ripe tomatoes

1 cucumber

1 bunch basil, stalks and leaves separated

¼ bunch mint, stalks and leaves separated

1 bunch coriander, stalks and leaves separated

½ bunch parsley, stalks and leaves separated

½ bunch chives, cut fine

400 grams overripe tomatoes

1 red chilli

Juice of 2–3 large lemons

2 cloves garlic

2 teaspoons Maldon salt

250 grams cracked wheat

Approximately 90 millilitres good olive oil

1 Plunge the firm tomatoes into boiling water, leave for 3 seconds and remove them to a bowl of iced water. Peel, quarter and deseed them, keeping all the peel, juice and seeds in a bowl. Cut the flesh into neat dice.

2 Cut the cucumber in half lengthwise and scoop out the seeds, adding them to the tomato seeds. Cut the cucumber into half lengthwise again twice, then cut across into small dice and add to the tomato.

3 Roughly chop the basil, mint, coriander and parsley leaves and toss gently into the tomato salad with the chives. Cover and refrigerate.

4 Liquidise the tomato seeds and peel with the overripe tomatoes, chilli, lemon juice, garlic, herb stalks and salt and pass through a sieve, pushing the debris with a ladle. Check for seasoning: it should taste salty and spicy.

5 Place cracked wheat in a bowl and pour in three-quarters of the liquid. Stir well and leave to soak for at least 1 hour in a cool place. Stir again adding the remaining liquid and some of the olive oil. It should look and feel moist though not runny.

6 Leave for another 30 minutes then gently fold in the tomato salad. Taste and add more lemon juice, olive oil or salt if necessary and serve.

SERVES 4

prawn and chicken pearl balls

Joy has given us two really fantastic authentic recipes. She advises that you can use chicken stock instead of water and that you can add one raw egg to the meat mixture for succulence. We don't mind telling you that we've eaten quite a few of these.

200	grams minced chicken thigh
200	grams minced raw prawn
1	spring onion, finely chopped
3	slices of ginger, finely chopped
2	teaspoons soy sauce
2	teaspoons oyster sauce
1½	teaspoons Chinese rice cooking wine
½	teaspoon salt
½	teaspoon chicken stock powder
½	teaspoon white pepper powder
1	tablespoon cornflour
2	tablespoons water
1	tablespoon sesame oil
150	grams sticky rice

1 Soak sticky rice in 250 millilitres water for 4 hours.

2 Put everything except sticky rice into a large mixing bowl and stir hard in the same direction for 5 minutes until well mixed.

3 Make 16 meatballs.

4 Drain the sticky rice.

5 Roll meat balls in sticky rice bowl, fully cover the meatballs with rice.

6 Put the rice balls in the steamer and steam for 20 minutes.

SERVES 4

In many ways our annual International Evening, the most loved of all events in the school calendar, is where the Fox Pot all began. One evening in September, when our brand new Reception children have just joined us and the new school term is drawing us all back together after the summer holidays, we gather around tables laden with food to celebrate the Fox melting pot.

fox sits down to eat

Sometimes we're in sunshine and sometimes rain (and on at least one memorable occasion, howling wind) but we're always surrounded by a riot of colour, national flags and costumes, and of course magnificent food prepared with care and a lot of pride by the families at Fox. The number of nationalities represented is staggering. Delicious smells fill the playground – everything from Lebanese Chicken, to Japanese Noodles, from Pork Buns to Tiramisu, from Aussie BBQ to French crêpes.

There is something magical about a group of people coming together with their children and extended families to share the food they love. Children try dishes they wouldn't dream of touching at home and parents who are perhaps a little quieter in the playground and prefer to stay in the background, suddenly come into their own. This feels like the beating heart of Fox; this is what we want our children to take with them all of their lives. This is the birthplace of the Fox Pot.

chicken satay with peanut sauce

There are several recipes in the book submitted by Zuraiha on behalf of her mother, Che Yah Ahmed, who even at 80 still rules the kitchen, both at home and at the nearby Malaysian High Commission. Here her grandson Aqeel reflects, "My Grandmother has been living with me since I was born making it almost 22 years to date, so I have quite an experience of being brought up with her food. There is something so magical about watching your grandmother in the kitchen. It is now our turn to take over and follow in her footsteps and, hopefully, teach the same to our grandchildren." Serve this with fluffy rice and cucumber. The chutney found in 'Sides' also complements it perfectly.

600 grams chicken meat
½ cup sugar
1 teaspoon salt
3 stalks lemongrass
Ginger (thumb size)
1 teaspoon turmeric

FOR THE SATAY SAUCE
500 grams peanuts
2 stalks lemongrass
50 grams brown sugar
50 grams white sugar
Salt to taste
4–5 cups water

1 Cut chicken meat into small chunks.

2 Put the ginger and lemongrass into a blender and blend.

3 Pour this into a bowl with the chicken. Mix in the rest of the ingredients and leave to marinate for at least an hour.

4 Insert the pieces of chicken onto skewers leaving about an inch and a half of room at the bottom of the skewer.

5 Cook on a barbecue or a grill until the chicken has fully cooked through.

SATAY SAUCE

1 Deep fry the peanuts in hot oil until brown and drain.

2 Mix the fried peanuts and the rest of the ingredients into a blender and blend until a smooth paste. Reduce or add water to desired consistency.

3 Cook this paste in a saucepan for about half an hour.

SERVES 4 TO 6

spaghetti and parmesan fritters

This recipe was given to Amy by an Italian nanny, pushing a toddler in a pram across the street in Notting Hill Gate. Her little boy was eating this amazing stick of spaghetti and she managed to give Amy the recipe while they stood on the island between green lights. It has become a family favourite. It's very easy to make, it's great for children's and teenagers' parties and is even good cold in lunch boxes. Amy serves it with a small bowl of fresh garlicky tomato sauce for dipping. But the best tip from Amy was to make the fritters into long stick shapes that can be bones to dip in the 'blood sauce' for Halloween.

3	large eggs
100	grams freshly-grated parmesan cheese
200	grams spaghetti, broken in half before cooking
	Salt and freshly ground black pepper
2	tablespoons olive oil
	Knob of butter

1 Cook spaghetti until al dente.

2 In a large bowl beat the eggs, grate in the parmesan and season liberally with salt and pepper.

3 Add to the cooked and drained spaghetti.

4 Heat the olive oil with a small knob of butter in a frying pan.

5 Add forkfuls of spaghetti and twizzle to form nice round shapes.

6 Fry until golden brown on both sides.

SERVES 2

spring rolls

A Hanh family favourite, this dish doesn't take long to make. You can get rice paper in specialist Asian shops. With a little bit of patience, small hands can help with rolling up the parcels. Even if not quite perfect, kids will love the results!

200	grams pork mince
½	onion
50	grams bean sprouts
20	grams vermicelli
50	grams carrots
40	grams mushrooms
2	eggs
25	rice papers
200	millilitres oil
1	spoonful chicken soup or stock

1 Mince the onion, bean sprouts, carrots, vermicelli, mushrooms and combine with the eggs and pork mince using your hands, until it becomes smooth.

2 Add chicken soup or stock and mix gently for 1 minute.

3 Soften the rice paper by covering with a clean damp cloth.

4 Roll one tablespoon of the mixture with rice paper, then put them into the boiling oil immediately.

Note: Instead of pork, you can use chicken or beef mince instead. The spring rolls should be crispy with a nice colour and aroma.

SERVES 4 TO 6

asparagus with tomato salsa and soft cheese

Chef and author Yotam Ottolenghi very generously sent us this simple and delicious recipe. His bright and vibrant Ottolenghi shop on Ledbury Road was his first and it's always full of locals. He and his business partner were brought up in Israel and Palestine, where the abundance of vegetables, pulses, grains and spices they were exposed to inform all of their cooking today. He tells us this dish is fantastic in the summer months. Bring on the sunshine.

½ small red onion

1 garlic clove, crushed

2 teaspoons white-wine vinegar

½ teaspoon aged balsamic vinegar

3 tablespoons olive oil, plus extra to finish

400 grams asparagus spears, woody bases removed

3 small ripe tomatoes (around 200 grams)

1 tablespoon dill, chopped

1 tablespoon parsley, chopped

1 tablespoon mint, chopped

100 grams soft and crumbly young cow's milk or goat's cheese

Maldon sea salt and black pepper

1 Cut the onion into 0.5 centimetre dice and place in a bowl along with the garlic, both vinegars, the olive oil and a pinch of salt. Stir, and then set aside so the onion and garlic will soften and mellow a little.

2 Make an ice bath by filling a bowl with ice and cold water. Bring a pan of water to the boil, drop in the asparagus and cook for two minutes. Drain, plunge the spears into the ice bath to stop the cooking, then drain and dry.

3 Heat a ridged griddle pan until almost smoking, then lay in a few spears at a time, perpendicular to the grill lines. Cook for two minutes a side, just until you get nice char marks, remove and leave to cool. Repeat with the remaining spears.

4 Quarter the tomatoes, remove and discard the seeds, and use a small, sharp knife to cut them into just under 1 centimetre square dice. Add the tomatoes and herbs to the marinating onion, season and stir gently.

5 Arrange the asparagus on serving plates and spoon the tomato salsa around their centre. Use your fingers coarsely to crumble the cheese and sprinkle over the salsa. Finish with a drizzle of olive oil over the tips and bases of asparagus, and possibly also a sprinkle of salt, depending on the saltiness of the cheese.

SERVES 6

steamed buns baozi

Joy makes 'millions' of these for International Evening and they are snaffled up. They also feature highly at the International Café at the School Fairs. She even held a Baozi making class in her home one morning. Of course we were all interested in learning, but even more keen on tasting! They are absolutely delicious. There is definitely a technique to making the perfect bun – but don't worry as they taste just as good if they look a bit wonky.

FOR THE BAOZI DOUGH

- 2 cups strong flour
- 1 cup (approx.) lukewarm water or milk
- 1 sachet dry fast-action yeast

FOR THE FILLING

- 1 tablespoon vegetarian oyster sauce
- 2–3 eggs, scrambled and finely shredded
- 1 teaspoon salt or to taste
- 2 spring onions, finely chopped
- 3–4 big slices fresh ginger, finely chopped
- 2–3 tablespoons sesame oil
- 3 bunches of spinach, blanched, finely chopped and water squeezed out
- 1 bunch glass noodles, soaked and cut finely
- 3–5 Shitake mushrooms, soaked to soften and finely diced
- 100 grams carrots, finely diced
- 50 grams dry tofu, finely diced

1 Make the dough. Mix yeast with flour and slowly add water. Knead the dough into a smooth ball. Cover the dough and let it rest for 2 hours till it doubles in size. It's better if you can knock it back (i.e. knock the air out of it) and leave to rise a second time.

2 Make the filling. Combine everything except the sesame oil and mix well. Then add sesame oil and mix again.

3 Make the wrap. Knead the dough until it forms a smooth ball then roll it into a sausage. Divide the dough into 12 small pieces. Roll each piece out into a circle. Place a small portion of the filling into the middle of each wrapper. Fold the dough over the filling into a half moon shape and pinch the edge to seal. To cook, put buns into steamer and steam on a high heat for 20 minutes.

SERVES 4

sesame prawn toasts

Hazel and her husband Daniel run Stick and Bowl on High Street Kensington. The restaurant was started originally by Daniel's father, Freddie Foo, as the takeaway arm of his brother's restaurant next door, the Fu Tong. Fu Tong was the darling of 1960s celebrities and Royals alike. Uncle Tong had a special cabinet where he kept personalised chopsticks for his frequent VIPs including Charlie Chaplin, Princess Margaret and Princess Anne. Even the late Princess Diana used to order the Chicken Chow Mein and Singapore Noodles. But why should the famous (and infamous) have all the fun? Here Hazel shares with us one of the most popular dishes of parents and kids alike.

2	slices white bread
100	grams raw prawns
1	egg white
1	mug vegetable oil
1	mug sesame seeds
½	teaspoon cornflour
½	teaspoon sesame oil
	Salt and pepper

1 Purée the prawns, egg white, sesame oil and cornflour until smooth, season well.

2 Spread the mixture on the slices of white bread.

3 Put the sesame seeds on a plate and press the pieces of bread spread with mixture into the seeds to coat.

4 Heat the oil and deep fry for about 3 minutes on each side until golden brown.

SERVES 2

woodland mushrooms on toast

This is the Cooper family's favourite holiday snack and, for them, just hearing about it evokes the rustle of autumn leaves. One of their favourite activities is mushrooming on the Isle of Purbeck, Dorset. They get up early, take their buckets to their secret location (sshh!) to find cep or chanterelle mushrooms. If they get lucky they might light up a little gas stove and have a picnic right there in the woods. Arthur and his brother Gabriel love them and have mushroomed since they were born. Enjoying this in London may mean forgoing the excitement of the hunt but if you are going to venture into woods take along a friend who knows what they are doing!

A few handfuls of ceps or any good, super-fresh mushrooms

A slice of butter

Glug of olive oil

Salt and pepper

4 slices good quality sourdough bread for toast

1 Wipe off any dirt from the mushrooms with a damp cloth.

2 Slice the mushrooms roughly while the butter and oil melt and heat in the pan. When the fat is just starting to bubble, throw in the mushrooms. Better to not let the pan get too crowded. You may have to do two pan-fulls if your pan is small.

3 Cook the mushrooms well, season to taste and let the juice slightly reduce in the pan.

4 Toast the bread and divide the mushrooms up.

SERVES 4

easy tomato soup

This is perfect when you return with hungry children from an over-ambitious (rainy) outing with no forward planning (most weekends!). On the whole there is always a tin of tomatoes at the back of the cupboard and that is practically all you need for this one.

1 tin tomatoes

Empty tomato tin filled with milk

1 level tablespoon flour

Knob of butter

1 teaspoon sugar

½ small onion

1 Bay leaf

1 Open the tin of tomatoes and tip it in the blender.

2 Fill the empty tinned tomato can to the top with milk and add to the blender.

3 Add the remainder of the ingredients and blend till smooth.

4 Pour into a saucepan and heat on the stove. After a few minutes the mixture will look like it has separated. Don't give up! Keep on cooking for another five or six minutes and the mixture will thicken. Taste for seasoning and serve with buttered toast.

SERVES 4

pink grapefruit soup with star anise
sopa de pomelo rosa con anís estrellado

When Jess, Barry and Jonty escape Notting Hill's weather, they head south towards Almeria, Murcia or any of those lovely Andalusian locations where rain is considered a climatic incident. Citruses are the kings of Iberica and this is a very refreshing palate cleanser. The unique and delicate fragrance of the star anise complements the tartness of the grapefruit and the richness of the Bourbon vanilla. In Jess's family, this soup is used in a very versatile way, before, during or at the end of a heavy dinner. It is also perfect at breakfast and brings sunshine to the table every single time.

6 large pink grapefruit

1 cup caster sugar

30 grams whole star anise

1 teaspoon pure vanilla extract

1 Bourbon vanilla pod

1 Segment the grapefruit into citrus suprêmes over a bowl. This is a simple method leaving beautiful segments without any skin. First, slice off the top and bottom. With a sharp paring knife, trim away skin and pith without removing too much flesh. Over the bowl, slip the blade along one segment until it reaches the core of the fruit. Turn the blade back on itself and slide it along the other side of the segment until it falls into the bowl free of any skin. Repeat for each segment as if you were flipping through a book. When all segments have been removed, squeeze the juices from the remaining core.

2 Gently mix sugar with the segments (preferably with your hands).

3 Slice vanilla pod lengthwise and remove seeds. Put the seeds and pod into the bowl, add the vanilla extract and mix thoroughly but gently.

4 Finally, add the star anise. Mix gently. Cover and let it rest in the fridge, ideally overnight. Serve chilled in soup bowls. Decorate with the star anise.

Variations: scoop out 3 or 4 passion fruit into the preparation.

The soup could be used as the base of a great dessert, grapefruit gratin, made with the drained segments. Put in an oven-proof dish, cover with sabayon and grill.

SERVES 4

fox garden mint jelly

1.8 kilograms cooking apples

1¼ cups water

450 grams caster sugar per pint of juice

1 big bunch fresh mint

1 Peel and core apples before cutting into pieces.

2 Put them into a large pan with the water and a few sprigs of mint. Stew slowly until soft and pulpy and test for pectin.

3 Turn into a jelly bag and leave overnight to strain.

4 The next day measure the juice, put it into a pan and add 450 grams caster sugar to each pint of juice.

5 Heat gently until the sugar dissolves. Bring to the boil and add the chopped mint (about two teaspoons per pint of juice).

6 Boil rapidly until the jelly sets when tested.

7 Put into jars and seal at once.

Note: To test for pectin put a teaspoon of the mixture onto a cold plate. It should go jammy and a finger wiped through it will leave a clean line that does not close up.

In 2007, Fox created an organic allotment. Tucked in the corner of the school behind the playground is a prolific garden with eight raised beds and a greenhouse that has successfully produced masses of vegetables for the past few years.

fox in the garden

This green garden is run on an eco-friendly drip system by our resident gardener, Jan De La Torre, and all the gardening is done by the children – every class from Year 1 to 5 gets a turn to garden regularly during the year in their science lessons. They grow an impressive range of organic vegetables including potatoes, carrots, lettuce, beetroot, chard, herbs, salad and lots of tomatoes. These vegetables go to the school kitchens to supplement mealtimes with fresh salads and any surplus is sold on a table for parents to buy in the summer months. Nina, the school chef, often cooks up a big batch of chutney from the late summer veg. which proves very popular at the Christmas Fair.

Many pots of mint jelly have been made by the children using the apples and mint from the school grounds and sold at the office. Here is the recipe for you to try (though we hope this doesn't dent the school's sales too much!).

andaluz butter bean stew with burnt garlic

Elisabeth Luard is an award-winning food writer, journalist and broadcaster. We're proud to say she's also a Fox grandmother and great supporter of the Fox Pot. This Luard family favourite is a creamy butter bean soup as they make it in Andalucía, home for much of Elisabeth's own children's childhood. It is simple, cheap and easy. No additional flavouring is required – no need for stock – and the juices will thicken naturally with the addition of olive oil at the end. If you soak a supply of beans for the freezer – a useful trick for all beans that need pre-soaking – you won't need to remember to put the beans in to soak the night before.

250	grams butter beans
½	whole garlic head
	Bay leaf
½	teaspoon peppercorns, crushed
2–3	tablespoons olive oil
	Salt

1 Soak the beans for at least 6 hours in enough cold water to cover generously.

2 Drain the beans and transfer to a roomy saucepan. Cover with twice their own volume of cold water, bring to the boil and skim off any grey foam that rises.

3 Meanwhile, push a knife into the half garlic-head and hold over a flame till blackened slightly, then rinse off any loose bits of blackened skin.

4 Drop the garlic-head into the beans with the bay leaf and crushed peppercorns – no salt. Bring back to the boil, turn down to a gentle simmer, put the lid on loosely and leave to cook gently for about 1½ hours, until the beans are perfectly soft. Check regularly and add more boiling water as needed.

5 When the beans are soft, remove the garlic and squish the insides into the soup. Add the olive oil. Bubble up so the juices form an emulsion with the oil.

6 To serve, either just leave it as it is – maybe lightly mashed – or, for a smooth soup, transfer everything to the liquidiser and whizz to a purée.

7 Reheat as necessary and ladle into bowls, finishing each serving with a swirl of olive oil and handing more for people to add their own. Possible extras are croûtons fried in olive oil with a little diced Serrano ham or bacon or garlic; a spoonful of pesto or chilli sauce; grated cheese (hand the grater around for everyone to add their own). Good with garlic bread and a green salad of peppery leaves.

SERVES 4 TO 6

ukrainian borscht

This is an old peasant soup that helped to keep up energy levels all year round. Traditionally, the recipe required pork ribs and lard, but it was adapted to reduce cooking time as well as fat. It can be cooked with beef ribs if preferred or would make a perfect vegetarian soup without any meat (but you might want to add more beans in tomato sauce to make it more filling). It is perfect served with rye bread and 1 to 2 tablespoons of sour cream on top and, if you like, one or two finely chopped cloves of garlic. The sour cream is always a must though!

3–4 boneless chicken thighs or 3 small chicken breasts (about 250 grams)

1 large or 2 small beetroot

4–5 medium white potatoes

1–2 medium size carrots

⅓ medium white cabbage

1 small white onion

2–3 tablespoons sunflower oil

3 bay leaves

1 can of beans in tomato sauce (small can of Heinz beans in tomato sauce works well)

3 tablespoons tomato paste

2–3 pinches of salt

1 Cut chicken meat into small pieces and put into 2 litres of water, bring to boil and cook for 10 minutes, add salt.

2 Add potatoes (cut into small cubes), cook until almost ready.

3 Cut beetroot into sticks, finely chop onion, carrots and cabbage.

4 Heat sunflower oil in a separate frying pan. Cook beetroot and carrots, then add chopped onions and cook until golden. Add tomato paste for the last 2 to 3 minutes of frying.

5 Add cabbage to the pot with meat and potatoes and cook together until cabbage is almost soft.

6 Add all the contents of the frying pan to the pot.

7 Add beans and cook for 3 to 4 minutes.

8 Turn off the heat and add bay leaves. Leave to stand for 10 minutes before serving.

SERVES 2

tarhana soup

This dish transports Sema straight back to her 'magical' childhood in Istanbul. Her mum made it often. It's hearty and satisfying but it's the tarhana that gives the soup its characteristic sour taste. The word is said to derive from 'dar hane', meaning poor house, as it was once served centuries ago to a sultan who called unexpectedly (as sultans do) at a peasant's house. The tarhana is a mixture of cracked wheat, yoghurt and vegetables and can be found in any Turkish or Greek food store.

4 tablespoons tarhana

500 millilitres beef stock

150 grams minced beef (optional)

150 grams butter

2–3 tomatoes

Salt, pepper and dried mint

1 Melt half the butter in a large saucepan.

2 Add the minced beef and cook until the juices evaporate, stirring from time to time.

3 Add the chopped tomatoes and cook for about 10 minutes. Add the meat stock and tarhana mixture.

4 Mix well and stir until it starts bubbling. Allow to simmer for 15 minutes on a medium heat.

5 Check seasoning and keep stirring. The soup will slowly thicken. You can adjust the consistency by adding more water.

6 Serve piping hot with dried mint and croûtons, made by slowly frying cubed bread with the rest of the butter in a pan.

SERVES 4

nettle soup

Adrian is the Chair of the Fox School Board of Governors and we're so grateful for the time and wisdom he has dedicated to the school over the years. He sent us this particularly interesting recipe for a soup made with stinging nettles. Probably best not to send the kids out to collect the ingredients for this one! Or if you do, then send them with some thick rubber gloves and a large supply of dock leaves. The flavour of the nettle is similar to spinach or sorrel and it's very rich in iron and chlorophyll and quite a lot of other nutrients as well – something of a 'superfood'.

25	grams butter
1	litre vegetable stock
1	medium onion, finely chopped
150	millilitres double cream
2	cloves garlic, crushed
	Freshly grated nutmeg
400	grams potatoes, diced
	Salt and black pepper
450	grams fresh nettle tops

1 Melt butter in a large pan.

2 Add the onion and garlic and cover. Cook until soft.

3 Add potatoes and nettles and cook for 2 minutes.

4 Add the stock, cover, bring to the boil and simmer for 15 minutes.

5 Cool a little before puréeing in a food processor.

6 Return mixture to clean saucepan and add cream, seasoning and nutmeg.

7 Reheat gently and serve.

SERVES 4

red lentil and orange soup with fennel seeds

This recipe was introduced to Anna by a dear friend many years ago and has since become a regular family favourite. Her children call it 'Orange Soup' and as long as she hides the ginger and they can squeeze the oranges, they'll eat it. Her five year old, Aliya, does complain about the fennel seeds but she wins her over by allowing her to add more orange juice. Vanya and even Niko, who is just one, are true fans.

1	litre fresh vegetable or chicken stock
1	leek, chopped
300	grams red lentils
1	piece fresh ginger, about 5 centimetres
4	oranges for juicing
1	tin plum tomatoes
2	tablespoons fennel seeds
	Salt and pepper
	A handful pearl barley (optional)
2	fresh tomatoes, chopped (optional)
	Olive oil

1 Rinse the lentils with cold water.

2 Peel the ginger and chop into very small pieces.

3 Juice the oranges (you may also add the fruit flesh – it's hardly noticeable in the soup and adds more flavour).

4 Fry the leek gently in a saucepan with olive oil until soft.

5 Add the lentils and fennel seeds and briefly fry together with the leek. Add pearl barley if using.

6 Add the stock to the lentils, leek and fennel seeds.

7 Add the tin of tomatoes (and optional fresh tomatoes if you like).

8 Add the ginger, salt and pepper.

9 Boil for about 20 minutes until the lentils are soft.

10 Add orange juice just before serving and stir in well.

SERVES 4

mains

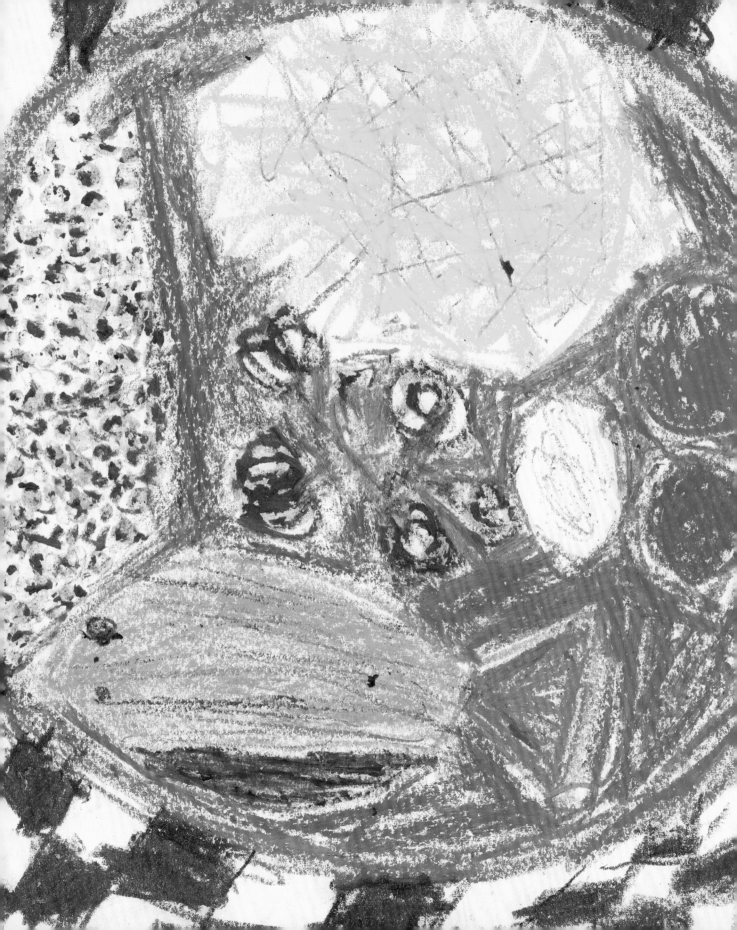

fish

parisian salt cod morue à la parisienne

In François's family, childhood memories were made of this type of dish, cooked for lunch by his grandmother Mamine and eaten religiously when school was off on Wednesday afternoons. He says that when they entered Mamine's flat, their school bags full of books and shoes full of the Parc Monceau's dust, he and his brothers were hooked by the indescribable smell of caramelised butter and garlic. They instantly knew they were in for a treat! This dish, though simple, is made more sophisticated by the different textures and tastes – the buttery crunchiness of the sautéed potatoes, the softness of the salt cod and the richness of the crème fraîche. This must be the ultimate schoolboys' reward!

600	grams Portuguese salt cod
800	grams yellow flesh potatoes (Charlotte or Vivaldi)
1	small bunch curly parsley
3	garlic cloves
1	litre fish stock
3	tablespoons crème fraîche
	Unsalted butter, olive oil (or goose fat)
	Salt and pepper

1 Depending on the nature of the salt cod, de-salt it in a large bowl filled with cold water over 24 hours and change the water at least twice (3 to 4 times is better).

2 Prepare the sautéed potatoes. Peel the potatoes then cut them in half lengthways then widthways in 5 millimetre slices.

3 In a large frying pan, heat the oil and butter or goose fat to a very high heat. Before the butter turns brown (or before the goose fat smokes), add the sliced potatoes. Add pepper from the mill and a little salt.

4 With a flat wooden spoon, mix well until all potatoes are well coated. Flip the potatoes to brown on each side.

5 When the potatoes are well coloured, turn the heat down and cover for 10 minutes to add some steam and cook through.

6 Remove the lid and continue cooking on a low flame until the potatoes are almost caramelised then remove from the heat.

7 In a large saucepan, bring to boil a court-bouillon (a mix of fish stock and water). Lower the heat and poach the sieved salt cod for 10 to 12 minutes until cooked.

8 Make a persillade by combining finely chopped parsley and garlic. Add to the potatoes.

9 Drain the salt cod and flake it over the warm sautéed potatoes. Mix gently. Put the frying pan back on a medium flame and mix in the crème fraîche. Serve immediately.

SERVES 4

bill granger | australia

glazed salmon with cucumber sesame salad

Australia's chef, restaurateur and author, Bill Granger has established an outpost in Notting Hill, Granger and Co., of his legendary Sydney restaurant, 'bills'. It has been phenomenally popular (note the queues up the street at most times of the day!). He says, "Salmon has a reputation for being the chicken breast of the fish world, and there's nothing wrong with that. Regarded as the healthy option, it's also packed with flavour, stands up to Asian ingredients and marinades beautifully. If you're bored with teriyaki, this is the recipe for you." We made it and it's really tasty. If you have a child who is a reluctant fish eater, this might be the dish to try.

FOR THE GLAZED SALMON

- 4 tablespoons mirin
- 4 tablespoons soy sauce
- 2 tablespoons brown sugar
- 1 tablespoon lemon juice
- 4 salmon fillets (about 175 grams each), skin off

FOR THE CUCUMBER SALAD

- 1 tablespoon mirin
- 1 tablespoon rice vinegar
- 1 teaspoon sesame oil
- 2 small cucumbers

1 Stir the mirin, soy sauce, sugar and lemon juice together in a bowl until combined. Put the salmon fillets in a shallow dish, pour the mixture over them and set aside in the fridge to marinate for 5 to 10 minutes.

2 Preheat a grill to high and line a grill tray with foil. Remove the salmon from the marinade, setting the marinade aside, and place the salmon on the tray. Grill for about 7 minutes, or until the fish is nicely coloured and still pink in the centre.

3 Meanwhile, pour the salmon marinade into a small frying pan and cook over high heat for 3 to 4 minutes until reduced to a glaze. Pour over the cooked salmon. Serve the glazed salmon with the cucumber sesame salad.

4 For the salad, whisk together the mirin, vinegar and sesame oil. Use a vegetable peeler or mandolin to peel long ribbons from the cucumber. Toss the cucumber ribbons with the dressing.

SERVES 4

Bill's Everyday Asian, Quadrille

hebridean pasta with fresh mussels

Lesley first made this dish in 2002 with her dear friend Christine Kozlov on the Isle of Jura, in the inner Hebrides after a walk during which everyone had filled their pockets with huge mussels. They've since cooked it at sunset while camping on a glorious beach near Arisaig and many times in London, though without the fun of collecting the mussels. If you do want to collect your own, be sure that the stretch of coast is unpolluted, and only pick large ones, leaving all small mussels to grow up. A sprinkling of chopped flat leaf parsley at the end is nice, though we're told that Lesley's children would disagree!

1	kilogram mussels, fresh if possible
4	tablespoons olive oil
2	cloves garlic, crushed
400	grams tin chopped tomatoes
500	grams spaghetti or linguine

1 First clean your mussels by scrubbing well and pulling out any beards. Discard any which do not close. This is a great job for children!

2 Heat a pan till very hot. Add the mussels, cover and shake. After a few minutes all the mussels should have opened, releasing their juices. Strain through a sieve, keep the juices and put the mussels aside, discarding any which haven't opened.

3 In a wide pan, gently sauté the garlic in olive oil, then add the tomatoes and the reserved mussel juices, and cook until the oil separates and the sauce is reduced and thick. Depending on your taste, you might like to add a half a cup or so of fish stock at this point.

4 Prepare the pasta to your taste and drain.

5 Just before serving add the mussels, removed from their shells, to the hot sauce to warm through. Do not cook further or they will become rubbery.

6 Mix the sauce through the pasta and eat – on the beach if possible.

Tip: This recipe also works well with clams and ready cooked mussel 'meat' from the supermarket.

SERVES 4 TO 6

monkfish armorican lotte à l'armoricaine

Lotte à l'Armoricaine was an all-time family favourite, lovingly made by François's grandmother Mamine (a woman who is fast becoming a legend among Fox Pot-ers) and the much beloved Annunziata, especially at New Year's Eve or at birthdays. François's family all smiled with anticipation around the pot until lifting the lid would uncover the much praised fish stew. Although it is a heart-warming dish, there is something definitely refined and delicate about it that always puts you in a party mood.

1.5 kilograms Atlantic monkfish tail (on the bone) cut in large pieces or steaks

250 grams onions

2 shallots

2 garlic cloves

1 bouquet garni

2 tablespoons flour

6 large vine tomatoes (in season) or 2 tins peeled tomatoes

1 tablespoon tomato paste

125 millilitres cognac (brandy)

500 millilitres Noilly Prat vermouth (white)

1 teaspoon sugar

2 tablespoons crème fraîche

Olive oil

Unsalted butter

Fresh tarragon

¼ teaspoon cayenne pepper

Salt and pepper

1 Finely chop the onions and shallots. On a medium flame, season and cook them in olive oil and butter until soft. Remove from the pot. Leave aside.

2 Season the monkfish pieces and add them to the pan. Colour them in olive oil on all sides then flambé with the cognac.

3 On a medium flame, add the onions and shallots, mix well and add the flour to the monkfish. Continue mixing on the flame and then deglaze with the vermouth.

4 Add the tomatoes and tomato paste, crushed garlic, bouquet garni, sugar, cayenne pepper and stir.

5 Bring it to the boil then simmer for about 25 to 30 minutes (do not overcook the fish!). Should the sauce be too liquid, remove the monkfish and reduce until it has thickened, then replace the pieces of fish.

6 Add the crème fraîche, stir on a low flame and add some finely chopped tarragon.

7 Serve immediately with white long grain rice.

SERVES 6

fried mackerel with ginger saba no tatsuta

John is a local and good friend of several Fox families. This recipe is one of the most popular family recipes in Japan and in his restaurant, Koya, customers sometimes order the second one right after they've eaten the first! Tatsuta is the shortened word for Tatsuta'age which means marinated and then fried, as opposed to Agebitashi which means fried and then marinated. Talk about 50 words for snow – the Japanese may have more than that for the ways they cook fish! Serve with green salad of watercress and lambs lettuce and if possible with homemade mayonnaise or remoulade.

2 large mackerel or 3–4 small mackerel, filleted, deboned and cut into the size of two mouthfuls.

FOR THE MARINADE

2 tablespoons soy sauce

1 tablespoon sake

1½ tablespoons mirin (sweet sake) or 1 tablespoon honey

1½ tablespoons ginger, grated

1 clove garlic, grated (optional)

2 spring onions, finely chopped

Pinch of dried chilli or shichimi spice (Japanese 7 spice)

Oil (any frying oil)

Potato starch or cornstarch

1 Make marinade, simply put all the ingredients together and marinate mackerel fillets for at least one hour. Marinate overnight, if you have time.

2 Prepare a frying pan with oil, deep enough to cover the fish. Heat it to 180°C.

3 Take out the fillets from the marinade, drain well, and coat with potato starch or corn starch. (Some chefs wipe off the marinade completely, but you don't have to do so. Just keep enough so that it makes a good batter with the starch – it will look like breadcrumbs in the end).

4 Now fry fillets until golden. Be careful not to burn. With the sugar content of marinade, it can easily get burnt and the fish over-cooked very fast. It is better to be under-cooked than over-cooked.

SERVES 4

sea bass with aubergine and rice

Sara gave us this really tasty and easy dish from Iran. It's quite simple and, without the extra chilli, would be a great meal for the whole family. The lime adds a zinging vibrancy to this lovely fresh dish.

6	sea bass fillets
630	millilitres hot vegetable or chicken stock
225	grams basmati rice
	Vegetable oil
1	onion, roughly chopped
1	large aubergine, cut in cubes
	Salt and black pepper
4	garlic cloves, crushed
	Juice of 2 limes
	Red chilli

1 Put rice in a sieve, wash until water runs clearly.

2 Brush an ovenproof dish with the oil then tip in the rice, onion and aubergine.

3 Season well.

4 Add other ingredients, except the fish.

5 Transfer to the oven and cook at 180°c for 30 minutes.

6 Lay the fish on top of the rice.

7 When the rice has absorbed all the stock and the fish is cooked through, it is ready to serve.

SERVES 6 TO 8

sweet and sour sea bream

You could use any white fish with a firm flesh for this recipe. For a dish so satisfying and full of flavour, this is surprisingly easy to make. If you prefer a healthier option you can steam or bake the fish rather than frying. Accompany with the rice and sambal (see page 131).

1 sea bream

½ cup tomato sauce

3 tablespoons chilli sauce

1 large white onion, sliced

½ teaspoon coriander

1 small chilli, finely chopped

Thumb-sized ginger, finely sliced

Turmeric powder

Salt and sugar to taste

1 Season the sea bream in salt and turmeric powder and leave for 10 minutes.

2 After 10 minutes, deep-fry the fish in oil until golden brown and set aside.

3 Heat oil in a wok and mix in the ginger. Fry for one minute.

4 Mix the rest of the ingredients into the wok and fry for 5 minutes.

5 Pour the sauce over the fried sea bream.

SERVES 4 TO 6

'what-belongs-to-the-fisherman' rice sayadiyeh

Sayadiyeh means "what belongs to the fisherman" – whatever fish was left over at the end of the day was taken home by the fishermen in Tripoli, Lebanon and their wives would make this dish. Diane who is a New Zealander, learned to make this dish by watching her mother-in-law, Teta Marie. Apparently, Teta Marie was generally recognised as the best cook in her huge extended family; she was so picky that she only ever ate food she had cooked herself. Teta Marie might have been horrified that we're giving away her secrets... but Diane's grandson Iskander and his little brother Laurie, adore this dish. Serve with the Tagen, provided by Tammy (Iskander and Laurie's Mum) on facing page.

FOR THE FISH STOCK

- 1 fish head and bones
- 1 litre water
- Bouquet garni, consisting of parsley stem, bay leaves (and other herbs)
- 2 lemon quarters
- 2 bay leaves
- 6 black peppercorns
- 1–2 sorrel leaves (optional)
- Salt to taste

FOR THE STEW

- 2 tablespoons olive oil
- 3 onions, finely chopped
- ½ teaspoon cinnamon
- ¼ teaspoon black pepper
- 500 grams monkfish tail, cut in medium-size pieces
- 1 teaspoon turmeric or four threads of saffron
- 280 grams rice
- Salt to taste

TO GARNISH

- 1 teaspoon olive oil
- 25 grams pine kernels
- 50 grams almond flakes

1 Place the fish bones and head into a pan, add the water and bring to the boil skimming until the water is clear. Add the bouquet garni and salt, reduce the heat to medium-low. Cover and simmer for 20 minutes.

2 Turn off the heat and let the pan stand for a further 20 minutes to intensify the flavours. Do not leave the stock simmering longer than 20 minutes.

3 In the meantime, place the oil in a medium-size pan, add the onions and fry until brown. Remove with a slotted spoon and put aside.

4 Fry the pieces of fish, then put aside. Now return the fish, rice and onions to the pan and add the stock. Bring to the boil, then reduce the heat to low. Cover and simmer for 8 to 10 minutes or until the rice is tender and the liquid has been absorbed.

5 Heat the oil and sauté the pine kernels and almonds until golden brown. To serve, place the rice in a dish, arrange the fish pieces on top and garnish with the pine nuts and almond flakes. Alternatively, add the fish pieces to the top of the rice pan while simmering so that the fish is finished by steaming rather than boiling.

SERVES 4

tammy boutel | **lebanon**

tahini onion sauce tagen

In Tammy's household they eat Sayadiyeh with a tahini onion sauce called Tagen. The secret to a good Tagen is to very slowly cook the onions until they are almost melting.

1 clove garlic, mashed

    Salt to taste

1 cup sesame paste (tahini)

¾ cup fresh lemon juice

¼ cup olive oil

½ cup fish stock

900 grams onions, halved and thinly sliced (not chopped)

    Pine nuts

    Parsley

1 Combine the mashed garlic, salt and sesame paste in a medium bowl. Add lemon juice and whisk until the mixture becomes a firm white paste.

2 Gradually add up to one cup of water whisking constantly until the mixture has the consistency of a heavy cream.

3 Heat olive oil in a pan over medium heat, add the onions and stir to coat. Reduce the heat to low and cook, stirring occasionally until most of the liquid has evaporated (about 10 minutes).

4 Simmer for about 15 minutes with ½ cup of fish stock until the stock is absorbed.

5 Drain the onions onto a paper towel and then add to the tahini mixture. Scatter with pine nuts and chopped parsley.

raw mackerel with sesame dressing

Local chef and seasonal produce champion, Valentine Warner sent us this delicious recipe. He advises that the mackerel for this recipe needs to be very fresh, stiff if possible, with that irides-cent green sheen not the dreary battleship grey colour. A very cleansing and fresh little dish – and also very healthy.

2 medium-sized mackerel, filleted and pin boned

FOR THE DRESSING

Double thumb-sized piece fresh root ginger, very finely chopped

2 small shallots, very finely chopped

2 cloves of good hard garlic (no green shoot in the middle)

2 finger length fresh red chillies, very finely chopped

1 teaspoon soft light brown sugar

1¼ tablespoons Japanese soy sauce, from a fresh bottle (do not use Chinese brands)

A few drops to taste of lemon

5 teaspoons sesame oil

1 Combine all the ingredients for the dressing and add a few drops of water if it appears a little dense. Give it a stir and allow to rest for 20 minutes or so.

2 Laying the mackerel skin side down on a board and starting from the tail, very thinly slice the fish on the diagonal, about 3 millimetres thick, tilting the back of the knife blade towards the thick end. Lay each mackerel fillet on a plate with the slices only just overlapping and spoon over the dressing. Eat immediately.

SERVES 4

danish fish balls with melted butter fiskefrikadeller

Britta, a Fox mum, designs gorgeous wedding gowns and owns the local business 'The Couture Gallery' on Campden Street. Her variation on traditional meatballs, replacing the meat with fish, makes a much lighter, healthier and fresher taste, a bit different from the usual meatballs. It's a light summer dish and is very easy and quick to make. Serve warm with boiled new potatoes sprinkled with parsley, melted butter and a mixed summer salad. Britta's children love them!

400	grams fillet of cod (or salmon)
1	teaspoon salt
1	small chopped onion
1	egg
2	tablespoons flour
150	millilitres milk
	Pepper
½	tablespoon oil
10	grams butter

1 Cut the fish into small pieces and mix together with salt, onion, egg, flour, milk and pepper. (You can also mix it together in a food-processor).

2 Heat butter and oil in a frying pan.

3 Shape the mixture into small balls using a hot tablespoon and place them in the pan.

4 Fry over a gentle heat until golden brown.

SERVES 4

spiced prawns

This recipe has been in Elsa's family for years. It's related to the 20 years that her parents lived in Mozambique, and it's one of the most appreciated in the family. She hopes everyone enjoys it as much as they do. This is such simple, delicious 'sunshine' food and goes beautifully with a salad and French fries. You could also thread the marinated prawns on skewers for a barbecue. Don't marinate for more than the recommended time though as the lemon juice will start to 'cook' the prawns and they will toughen up.

1 kilogram tiger prawns, raw and shelled

Salt

2 large (or 3 small) lemons

Butter

Spice (e.g. cayenne, Ras El Hanout or other spice mix)

1 First of all, the prawns need to be prepared and seasoned. Start by making a deep cut all the way through the back of each prawn, in order to remove the brownish-black threads. Next, rinse the prawns and pat them dry with kitchen paper.

2 Season the prawns with salt and the juice of 2 or 3 lemons, depending on the size of the lemons and on each one's taste. Add some spice. Leave them to rest for 3 hours.

3 Preheat the oven to 200°c. Place the prawns in a shallow baking tray together with the marinade. Spread small shells of butter on the top of the prawns (don't worry too much about the precise quantity, just put it on according to your taste).

4 Place the tray in the centre of the oven for about 15 minutes, until the prawns turn to the reddish prawn colour.

5 For the lemon butter sauce, melt one tablespoon of butter, take away from the heat and add the juice of one lemon. Pour onto the prawns in each dish, if desired.

SERVES 4

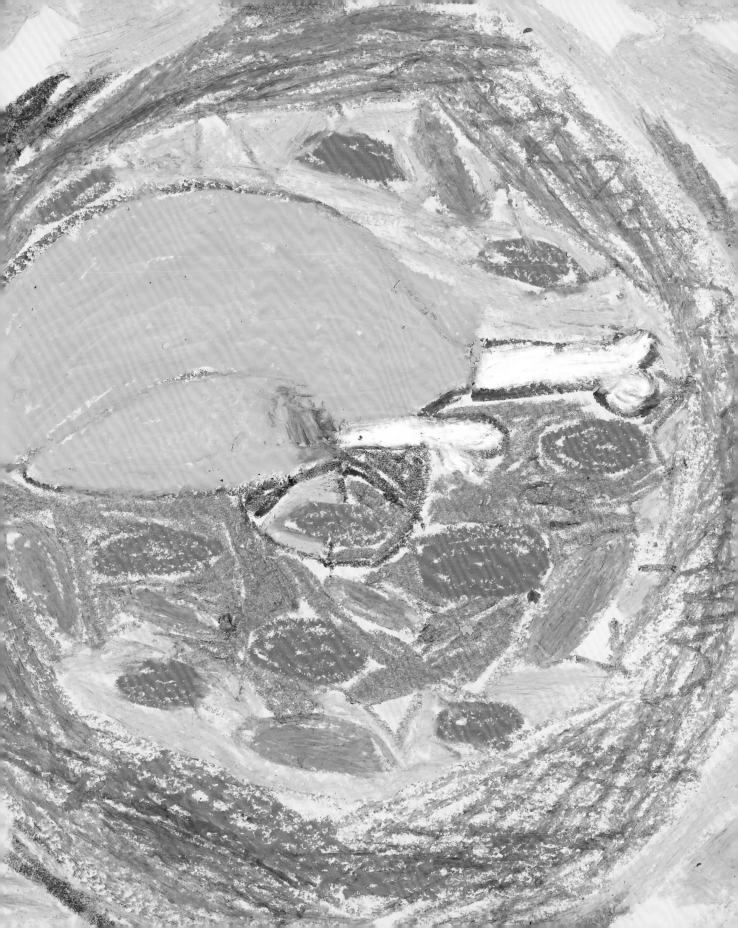

poultry

caesar salad with grilled chicken

Nina has been Head Chef at Fox for as long as anyone can remember. She is our very own Nigella Lawson and her meals are delicious. New parents are always given the opportunity to join their children for lunch so they can sample her cooking. We asked her to give us the recipe that most children name as their favourite – and this was it. It certainly surprised some of us whose children won't even entertain the idea of eating a lettuce leaf at home! Incidentally, unless you are holding a party for 260 children (not something anyone would recommend) you might want to adjust the quantities. Nina serves this with new potatoes, or couscous salad, and broccoli.

20	kilograms chicken thighs
10	heads cos lettuce
4	loaves of bread (for croûtons)
1.2	litres Caesar dressing (either bought or use our recipe)
6	teaspoons paprika
6	teaspoons salt
3	teaspoons black pepper, ground
290	millilitres vegetable oil

FOR THE CAESAR DRESSING

600	grams parmesan, grated
8	tablespoons white wine vinegar
1	litre mayonnaise
12	tablespoons Dijon mustard
8	anchovy fillets, rinsed
1	teaspoon salt
4	garlic cloves, crushed
200	millilitres olive oil

1 Mix the seasoning with the vegetable oil to make a paste and mix with the chicken (can leave in the fridge overnight if you wish but you don't have to).

2 Chop the lettuce, wash and spin to dry.

3 Cut the bread in cubes, mix with a little vegetable oil and roast in a hot oven, till golden brown. Leave to cool.

4 Cook chicken in a very hot pan or grill, five minutes on both sides or until cooked.

5 When chicken is ready, leave it to cool then mix, with the croûtons, into salad and dress.

THE DRESSING

Mix all ingredients in a bowl and give it a good whisk until incorporated. Or you could put everything into a large container with a lid and shake, shake, shake!

SERVES 260

pigeon breasts with fennel

This is an easy, yet sophisticated dish that Alison's son Arthur created one evening and has become a family staple. You can substitute chicken breasts if pigeon is not for you. It is perfect served with Puy lentils and rice.

Pack of pigeon breasts from the butcher or farmers' market or four chicken breasts sliced into smaller pieces

1 large fennel bulb

2 garlic cloves (optional)

2 slices butter

2 tablespoons olive oil

A handful chopped flat leaf parsley

A handful chopped fennel tops

Salt and black pepper

½ glass dry white wine (optional)

½ glass vegetable or chicken stock

1 Peel and finely slice the garlic and fennel. Reserve the feathery fennel tops.

2 Put the oil and butter in the pan and bring to a medium heat, add the fennel and garlic. Let them soften, stirring repeatedly. When completely soft and translucent, season with salt and pepper. Remove the fennel from the pan and place on a warm plate.

3 Put the pigeon or chicken breasts in the pan with a little more oil. Put the heat up a touch. Once the breasts are nearly cooked (after five minutes or so), season and pour in the wine and stock. Let it bubble and reduce slightly.

4 Serve the pigeon breasts on top of a bed of fennel sprinkled with the parsley and fennel tops.

SERVES 4

chicken and rice arroz con pollo

It was Jack, Guy and Charlie's Abuela who sent this recipe to us from the United States. It's served on all special occasions in Puerto Rico, usually with red kidney beans and fried plantains on the side. It has a strong flavour but is not too spicy. If you can't get hold of achiote (we picked ours up at The Spice Shop on Blenheim Crescent) you can substitute turmeric. Achiote is known as the poor man's saffron so if you feel like splashing out you could use that instead. A little coriander and a wedge of lime at the end are also nice for a change.

1 kilogram chicken thighs with skin

2 yellow onions

3 garlic cloves

3 tablespoons extra virgin olive oil

½ cup coriander seeds

2 tablespoons dried oregano

1 tablespoon salt

½ cup capers

2 tablespoons achiote (annato) seeds

2 cups white rice

1 large jar pitted stuffed olives

1 jar red pimentos

1 With a mortar and pestle, crush together the garlic, coriander seeds, salt, oregano.

2 Add capers.

3 Marinate chicken in this for 2 to 3 hours.

4 Heat the achiote seeds in oil until red. Remove seeds with slotted spoon and discard.

5 Fry chicken in achiote oil till browned. Remove chicken from pan and set aside.

6 Add diced onions, rice and cook gently in the oil until rice is cloudy.

7 Add to the rice the chicken, marinade liquid mixture, olives and 3 cups water. Bring to the boil and simmer covered on stove or in oven for 30 minutes.

8 Garnish with pimentos.

SERVES 6

persian sweet and sour chicken fesenjoon

Aida Valentina sent us a couple of really lovely recipes. This one is delightfully sweet and should please most children. We picked up pomegranate concentrate and Persian saffron from the Iranian grocer at the west end of Kensington High Street. You really can't substitute with pomegranate juice unfortunately – it doesn't taste right at all. A great accompaniment would be Persian rice – cooked the proper Persian way, rinsing then soaking the rice for two hours beforehand and then adding a little saffron and oil to the cooked rice.

1	large chicken (ask butcher to chop it into 10 pieces on bone)
1	onion, finely chopped
180	grams walnuts, finely crushed
¼	teaspoon ground black pepper
¼	teaspoon ground turmeric powder
¼	teaspoon ground mild curry powder or garam masala (optional)
¼	teaspoon ground Persian saffron
1	cup of sugar
1	litre hot water
250	millilitres pomegranate purée/concentrate
	Oil of your choice

1 Heat the oil in a large non-stick pot or casserole.

2 Fry chopped onion until it's golden brown.

3 Add chicken pieces and stir together with the onion.

4 Season with black pepper, salt, turmeric and curry powder and stir.

5 Add saffron and keep stirring until the chicken turns golden brown then add the sugar.

6 Tip in the walnuts and pomegranate concentrate.

7 Pour hot water into the pot, stir again.

8 Make sure the sugar has dissolved and bring to the boil.

9 After 5 to 8 minutes reduce the heat and let it simmer until the sauce is reduced and thickened and the colour changes into a dark brown.

SERVES 4 TO 6

curried chicken rice tsebhi birsen

The kitchen of an Eritrean household is something to behold – the sizzle, the bustle and the over-whelmingly pungent smell of spices frying. Muna was taught this recipe by her mother when she was younger. It was one of her favourite dishes – she always helped her mother cook it for dinner. Now she cooks it for her children and her youngest Tawfeeq, loves it the most. It's quick and easy and can be eaten on its own or with different toppings like salad or yoghurt. The scent and flavour of cassia and cardamom in this recipe are a revelation. Continuing the tradition, Muna is now teaching this to her two older daughters so that her grandchildren (one day) can enjoy it too!

1   baby chicken, jointed into 8 pieces

4   cups basmati rice

2   onions

3   tablespoons vegetable oil

2   teaspoons curry powder

6   cloves (optional)

½   Natco cassia stick

7   green cardamom pods

Salt

Tomato paste

1 Chop the onions and add to the sizzling oil.

2 Mix together and allow to simmer.

3 Add the chicken.

4 Add curry powder, cassia stick, cloves and green cardamom.

5 Add tomato paste.

6 Mix and brown for 10 minutes.

7 Add salt and 1 cup of hot water – leave to simmer for 10 to 15 minutes.

8 Add 4 cups of water.

9 Wash the rice and add to the chicken then cook on high for 10 minutes.

10 After the sauce reduces, leave on low heat for 20 minutes before serving.

Note: Natco cassia sticks are available from halal shops or The Spice Shop on Blenheim Crescent.

SERVES 4 TO 6

fried chicken in hot tomato sauce

This is a dish that Abi regularly cooks for her family. With a little preparation the day before it cooks up quickly. It is pretty hot though, that's how Abi and her family like it, but you may want to modify the spice. Abi says she serves this dish with either boiled potatoes, French bread or basmati rice and some steamed vegetables.

500 grams chicken thighs or drumsticks

800 grams tinned chopped tomatoes

3 garlic cloves, crushed

1 tablespoon salt

1 teaspoon black pepper

1 teaspoon chilli powder

2 onions, peeled and roughly chopped

2 tablespoons tomato purée

1 tablespoon olive oil

1 chicken stock cube

1 teaspoon paprika or cayenne pepper (optional)

1 Marinate and season chicken with salt, pepper, garlic, sprinkle paprika or cayenne pepper and leave overnight in the fridge.

2 Grill the chicken until it is golden brown and cooked through, turning every now and then.

3 Put the oil in a frying pan adding onions and garlic and cook until soft. Add chopped tomatoes and tomato purée. Season to taste.

4 Stir on a medium heat for 10 minutes.

5 Place chicken in an oven tray and pour the cooked tomatoes over it until all the chicken is covered. Place in the oven for 15 minutes at 190°C.

SERVES 4 TO 6

Everyone loves a party and Notting Hill Carnival is Europe's largest. It started in 1964 as a way for London's Afro-Caribbean communities to celebrate their traditions and cultures and Fox has been a part of the Carnival, contributing artwork and performing, since 1997. A pretty homespun group at first, they've grown to become bona fide contenders for prizes. Throughout it all however they've always embodied the true spirit of carnival – families coming together in celebration, rather than professional dancers in elaborate costumes. The "band" refers to a band of dancers, there aren't actually any instruments (though a bit of singing is always welcome).

fox loves carnival

Families set off from Fox early in the morning, dancing behind a huge sound system as the traffic is held back to let them pass. Crowds line the streets to wave and cheer – it's a pretty joyous sight! When the group reaches the official Carnival route, they pause and set out the tables. Ah yes – there had to be some food involved! Samosas and Caribbean chicken are laid out beside cupcakes and sweets. It's certainly enough to shore up energy for the dance-athon that follows.

What really makes Fox Carnival float so special is the uniqueness and vibrancy of each individual piece of art and the person carrying it. There are no complicated dance moves but lots of enthusiasm as everyone follows the band leader (since the very beginning, our own irrepressible Captain Danceheart, Colin Salmon). As one carnival participant put it, "I came as an immigrant to London as a small child and I've lived here all my life but it wasn't until I danced through the streets as part of the Fox Carnival that I felt that this was my community and these were my streets."

bolivian chicken and chocolate picante

Annie's daughter Anahi was a chair of the Fox School Association when her two children were at the school. She put an enormous amount of energy into the school and is remembered with a lot of affection by everyone. This recipe from her mother Annie was submitted to us over several pages with wonderful descriptions of how this was prepared in Bolivia and where to buy the ingredients in London (right down to parking tips!). It was so fabulous we decided to reproduce the pages here. Annie suggests that, as with all stews, leave it a day and it will have amalgamated.

1 chicken, jointed

Aji

2 onions, chopped

6 cloves garlic, chopped

2 red peppers, chopped

1 teaspoon oregano, heaped

1 teaspoon cumin

A handful coriander, chopped

Salt and pepper

1 litre water

Dark chocolate

1 chicken stock cube

1 handful breadcrumbs

1 Chop onions, garlic and red peppers and fry slowly for about 20 minutes.

2 Mix together with Aji and pour into a pot.

3 Add oregano, cumin, coriander, salt and pepper.

4 Add water and boil gently for 5 minutes.

5 Grind chocolate and add.

6 Add the chicken and boil the whole lot for about 45 minutes to 1 hour.

7 Put 1 chicken stock cube into the pot.

8 At the end sprinkle breadcrumbs to thicken the sauce.

SERVES 4 TO 6

Picante de pollo

Annie COPPONEX

chicken cooked in a sauce served with:

RICE — 1 potato — chuño phuti — sarsa

Rice — plain

potatoes boiled

Sarsa: finely sliced onions and finely sliced tomatoes, tossed together w/ some salt, this sauce will be sprinkled over

chuño phuti: these are dehydrated potatoes. (The incas conserved potatoes this way in case of famine....

The day before soak chuño... next day cut in pieces boil about 15 min. drain — make a mixture of 1 whipped egg and some grated Cheshire or Lancashire or Caerphilly white cheese. Also finely chop and fry till transparent 1 bigish onion pour all this over the drained chuño. Cover and just warm a bit. Do not bring to boil... The heat of chuño will cook this mixture. For us, this is a delicacy [my english friends also love it however they say it tastes like old socks !!]

Picante de pollo.

chicken Thighs are the best. (it's always good to have meat with BONES — The sauce is richer)

X you will need AJI (hot peppers.)

oregano, cumin, coriander leaves, chocolate, bread crumbs

onions, garlic

chop: 1-2 onions

" 6 cloves garlic

" 2 red peppers

fry: slowly + steam for 20 min.

mix: together w/ aji mush →

pour: into pot all this mush

add: 1 tbs heaped — oregano

1 ~~coriander~~ cumin

1 handful chopped coriander

salt, pepper add water

boil gently 5 min... grind chocolate 1-2 pints and add

chicken — Now boil the whole lot for about 45 min — 1 hr. put 1 chicken broth cube into juice. See that chicken is done.

stews leave till next day X it will have amalgamated

Day before wash and boil for 10 min. a handful of AJI (hot peppers (these are dried — need soaking and soak overnight). Next day open a remove pips, cut in pieces and put into sterizer zap w/ a bit of water. Make mush

—

At end sprinkle bread crumbs to thicken sauce

Anahi says you can buy aji at the Chil. company on Blenheim cresent. I enclose some samples. AJI, CHUÑO, CHOCOLAT Do not use chilly powder or cayenne powd it does not taste right.

There is a shop on the Old Kent Road (go on it's an adventure)

SOL ANDINO
187 Old Kent Road   SE1 5NA
73 94 9203   mob 07507 633 245

(do not park on the small dead end street — Marcia Rd. is OK !! (next) and close to shop.

LEFT Over flyover a small parade w/ lots of shops — it's next to a hairdresser — across the street is ALDI or LIDL?

—

In the shop — you can get AJI, CHUÑO, buy SALTEÑA (Cornish pastry like !! Delicious)

For dessert we sometimes have white cheese like Caerphilly Lancashire etc. with a slice of GUAYABA thick jelly similar to quince jelly. this is lovely and you can buy it. There is bolivian coffee — argentine dulce de leche — they also have some lovely white corn on the cob with great big kernels.

—

I always have some of the sauce if you want some call me I'm happy to help — am not going anywhere for the holidays

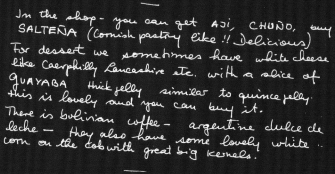

coronation chicken

Emily and her family had this for lunch to celebrate the royal wedding! She says it's very easy and pretty much foolproof. The famous English recipe, originally called Poulet Reine Elizabeth, was created by the founder of the Cordon Bleu cookery school, Rosemary Hume, for the banquet of the coronation of Queen Elizabeth II. It was popular under rationing and is still an old favourite for summer entertaining. Serve with basmati rice and a green salad.

1 whole chicken

5 peppercorns

1 teaspoon salt

5 tablespoons mango chutney

50 grams dried apricots or 1 tablespoon of apricot jam

2 tablespoons curry powder

2 teaspoons Worcester sauce

200 millilitres mayonnaise

200 millilitres natural yoghurt

50 grams flaked almonds

Fresh coriander

1 Simmer chicken in a large saucepan with peppercorns and salt. Cook for about one and a half hours until the juices run clear.

2 Take the chicken out of the pan and, when lukewarm, remove the meat in small pieces.

3 Mix the chutney and the apricot pieces or jam into a large bowl.

4 Toast the curry power in a dry frying pan and add to the mixture.

5 Add the mayonnaise, yoghurt and the Worcester sauce to the mixture.

6 Stir the chicken into the mixture.

7 Put into the fridge for a couple of hours.

8 Add some chopped coriander and a sprinkle of dried almonds.

SERVES 6

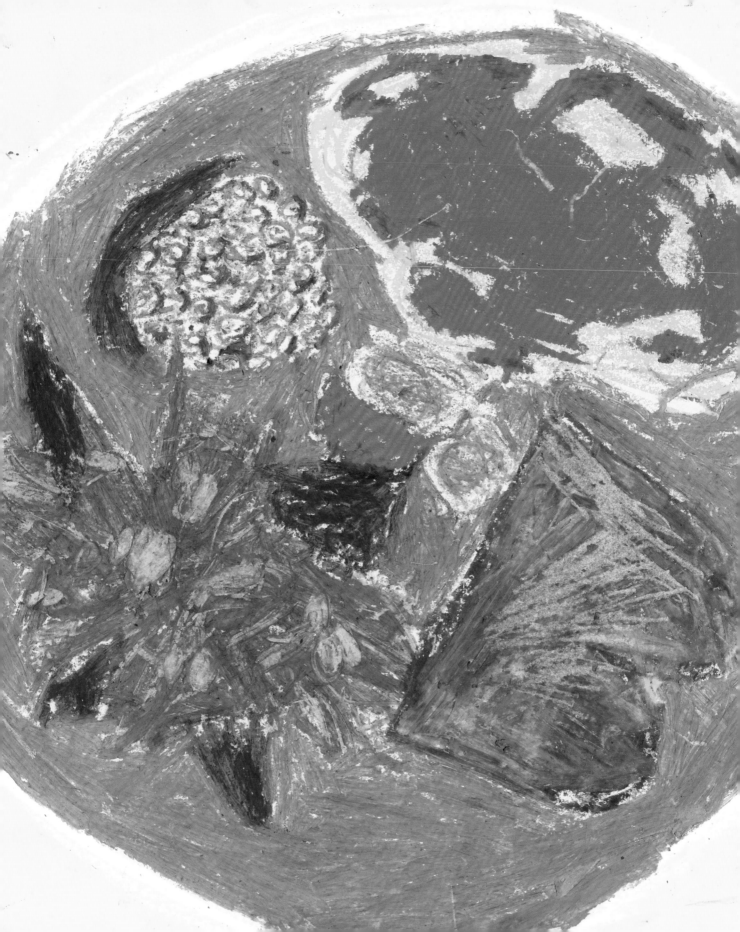

meat

crispy roast pork belly

This is a very popular hawker dish. It is commonly served with rice, sometimes together with other roasts like roast duck. Chai brought this for us to taste at one of our Fox Pot meetings. It was succulently divine. Now we all go slightly misty-eyed when anyone mentions the 'crispy roast pork belly morning'. Serve the pork with fluffy jasmine rice.

1 Belly pork joint – a piece of belly joint, at least 10 x 20 centimetres

Salt

Five-spice powder

1 Rub the five-spice powder into the meaty side of the joint.

2 Score the skin with criss-cross lines. Sprinkle a generous layer of table salt over the skin side of the joint.

3 Leave uncovered in the fridge overnight.

4 Preheat oven to 240°C.

5 Dust or wipe off excessive salt from the skin.

6 Make a tripod with a tin foil tray. Lay the piece of joint over the tripod, ensuring that it is stretched.

7 Roast for 40 minutes, (the signs of successful crackling are browning and bubbling of the skin). If skin is not evenly crisp, reposition the piece such that the less crisp section is placed on top part of the tripod. Then roast for another 10 to 20 minutes.

8 Rest the roast for 30 minutes before serving with rice.

SERVES 3 TO 4

cool souvlaki with pork strip in rice paper

The new Greek restaurant in Notting Hill, Mazi, sits just up from Fox on Hillgate Street, on the site of the legendary Costas Grill. Award-winning chef, George Venieris, says, "Taking traditional recipes and transforming them with a modern twist is what we are all about." This gorgeous recipe is one of their most iconic dishes, and represents Mazi's philosophy: a classic popular dish in Greece revamped with a bit of modern imagination. This dish is perfect to share with friends and family, easy to make but guaranteed to impress.

FOR THE PORK

400	grams pork belly
2	grams oregano
3	teaspoons Dijon mustard
1	red onion, chopped
	Salt and pepper
2	grams sweet paprika

FOR THE MUSTARD WATER

2	teaspoons Dijon mustard
300	millilitres water
2	garlic cloves
1	teaspoon oregano

FOR THE CARAMELISED ONIONS

1	red onion
10	grams olive oil
20	grams sugar
10	grams red wine vinegar

FOR THE WRAP

	Rice paper wraps
1	tomato
10	grams parsley
1	red onion
	Salt and pepper
	Oregano

1 Place the pork belly on an oven tray. Add paprika, oregano, pepper and mustard and onion. Add water till the pork is completely submerged. Cover it with parchment paper and aluminium foil and cook at 170°c for approximately 4 hours. When ready let it cool down.

2 Prepare the mustard sauce by mixing all the ingredients thoroughly.

3 Cut the red onion into strips. Place in a pan and cook with olive oil until soft. Add the sugar and the red wine vinegar and cook until caramelised. Julienne the tomato.

4 Soak two pieces of rice paper in the mustard sauce mix until soft. Remove and place them, wide open, on a chopping board. Meanwhile cut the cooked pork into strips and place in a hot pan. Add some dried oregano and sweet paprika powder. Cook until crispy.

5 In the middle of each rice paper place the tomato, caramelised onion, parsley, pork, salt and pepper. Roll it like a wrap making sure both sides are closed. Leave to dry for 5 minutes. Cut the roll in half and serve at room temperature.

6 Serve your wraps with garlic yoghurt sauce on a bed of sliced cucumbers. For this, simply mix 100 grams of Greek yoghurt with 20 millilitres of olive oil and a finely chopped clove of garlic. Add salt and pepper. Cut 1 cucumber in half lengthwise and cut it in juliennes. Add 50 grams of rocket and a home-made vinaigrette.

SERVES 4 AS A STARTER

melting chinese pork dong po rou

This recipe is over nine hundred years old. For Cordelia, former Fox teacher, who's considerably younger than that, it evokes strong memories of her childhood. "This melt-in-your-mouth dish is always one that jumps into my mind whenever I miss my mum's cooking. There is something so comforting about being instantly transported to Mum's kitchen at the first scent of pork roasting. Whether it be the juicy tenderness or the simple, yet rich and fragrant sauce – it's a real winner every time."

1   kilogram pork belly with skin on

    Kitchen string

2   tablespoons brown sugar

2½ cups shaoxin wine (Chinese rice wine)

4   pieces star anise

1   stick of cinnamon, about 8 to 10 centimetres

3   thick slices fresh ginger

4   stalks spring onion, white part only

1   cup water

2   tablespoons dark soy sauce

3   tablespoons light soy sauce

1 Blanch pork belly in boiling water for 2 minutes and drain.

2 Cut the pork belly into cubes of 4 centimetres by 4 centimetres and tie with kitchen string, as you would tie ribbon around a present.

3 Use a heavy-based pot big enough to hold the pork parcels in a single layer and place them skin side down; put all dry ingredients in the pot.

4 Make sure the rice wine covers ⅔ of the pork then add enough water to just cover the top of the pork.

5 Cook for 35 minutes then turn the pork parcels skin side up.

6 Bring to a gentle simmer, reduce heat and cover tightly. Leave it to cook for at least 3 hours or longer until the meat is tender. You can also cook it in the oven at 170°C.

7 Remove string before serving with steamed rice.

Note: The Dong Po pork flavour depends very much on the quality and flavour of the soy sauces used, so make sure you use good ones.

SERVES 6

beef and pork meatballs

How many recipes throughout history have been created to disguise vegetables or get children to eat more adventurously? This recipe was created to do both. You can easily miss out the paprika if that's a flavour too far for your kids. In this case, the carrots not only provide some hidden nutrition they also make the dish lighter than if it were all meat. Georgina and her family like to tuck into this after a windy walk on the beach at the Isle of Wight. It's a delicious warming dish, enjoyed by kids and adults alike.

FOR THE MEATBALLS

250 grams lean minced beef

250 grams free range pork mince

1 onion, finely chopped, sweated down in olive oil

A handful flat leaf parsley, chopped

2 carrots, finely grated

Salt and pepper

FOR THE SAUCE

1 tin chopped tomatoes

1 tin cannellini beans

1 tablespoon tomato purée

A handful flat leaf parsley, chopped

1 onion, finely chopped, sweated in olive oil

1 beef stock cube

1 teaspoon smoked paprika (optional)

Olive oil

1 In a bowl mix the meatball ingredients and then form into balls about the size of a golf ball. Fry them on all sides in olive oil until lightly brown.

2 Put all the sauce ingredients except the cannellini beans into a large casserole dish. Bring to the boil.

3 Once the meatballs are cooked add the cannellini beans to the tomato sauce, stir then add the meatballs carefully so that they do not break up. Simmer gently in the casserole dish for about an hour.

4 Serve with spaghetti or rice with a good sprinkling of parmesan.

SERVES 4

texas chilli bean cook-up

Make this as hot as you like! Spoon it over rice and add any other toppings you desire. You could eat it around the campfire *Blazing Saddles*-style if you like or failing that, in front of the TV watching *Blazing Saddles*. Enjoy!

500 grams mince steak

1 large onion, chopped

1 red or green mild capsicum (bell pepper), chopped into bite-size chunks

2 cloves garlic, chopped

1 teaspoon oregano

1 teaspoon cumin powder

3 tablespoons chilli powder

Cayenne red pepper ($\frac{1}{8}$–1 teaspoon to taste)

Salt and pepper to taste

2 tins chopped tomatoes

1 tin or carton red kidney beans (in chilli sauce even better)

OPTIONAL TOPPINGS

Plain yogurt or sour cream

Grated cheddar cheese

Pickled jalapeños

1 Using a large pot, cook the mince, onions, peppers and garlic until the mince is cooked through.

2 Drain off the grease.

3 Add spices and tomatoes and let simmer for five minutes.

4 Add kidney beans toward the end, just so they heat through. Add your choice of toppings.

SERVES 4 TO 6

christina bartholomew | **usa**

grilled flank steak with salsa and caramelised onions

This is one of the Bartholomews' favourite recipes to share with guests. The flavours are surprising, fun and just taste good together. And it's easy to get the kids involved. Julian, the youngest, de-stems the coriander while Aidan and Nathaniel take on chopping duties. "Entertaining has changed dramatically now that the kids are growing up," says Christina. "We used to put them to bed before dining with guests. Now, they often join the adults at the table, contributing conversation, funny stories and a good bit of chaos."

5 onions, sliced

Generous puddle of extra-virgin olive oil

1½ kilograms flank steak or bavette

FOR THE STEAK RUB

1 teaspoon salt

1 teaspoon garlic powder

1 teaspoon dried oregano

1 teaspoon black pepper

½ teaspoon ground cumin

FOR THE SALSA

⅔ cup vegetable broth

½ cup fresh coriander, chopped

½ cup red onion, chopped

½ cup red pepper, chopped

¼ cup white wine vinegar

¼ cup extra-virgin olive oil

1 teaspoon salt

1 teaspoon dried oregano

1 teaspoon dried chilli flakes (or to taste)

½ teaspoon black pepper

4 garlic cloves, chopped

1 Start by caramelising the onions—sauté gently in olive oil over low to medium heat (adding salt and pepper from time to time) until the onions start to brown. Take your time, the slower the better. You can help them along with a pinch of sugar if you like.

2 Meanwhile, cover all sides of the flank steak with the rub. Let sit until the meat reaches room temperature.

3 Mix all the salsa ingredients in a bowl and refrigerate. This yummy, colourful salsa can be prepared the day before and keeps for several days thereafter.

4 Grill the steak to rare. Let sit for a few minutes to bring up to medium rare. Slice against the grain. Rib eye, sirloin and filet mignon work well too.

5 Serve steak strips alongside a spoonful of red camargue rice and a dollop of the caramelised onions. Top the lot with your copious spoonfuls of salsa.

SERVES 6

The year 1936 is stamped into the bricks of the Fox School building, but the story of Fox dates back nearly one hundred years before that to the passion and progressive philosophies of the Right Honourable Caroline Fox. Sister to the third Lord Holland and aunt to the fourth and last, she was born in 1767. Though the famous philosopher and reformer Jeremy Bentham, proposed to her, she never married. Along with her nephew she fought hard for the abolition of slavery. She was known as a highly-respected, intelligent and thoughtful woman, with strong liberal views – a Fox woman indeed!

the fox story

In 1842, near the end of her life, Caroline Fox established a charity school on the north side of Holland Park Road, "for the education of children of the labouring, manufacturing and other poorer classes of Kensington", and when she died she left money to ensure its upkeep. Eventually, newly established School Boards took over the school and moved it to Kensington Church Street, then called Silver Street after its thriving silver trade. When Silver Street's burgeoning crowds, arriving via its new underground stations, required plans for widening, Fox school had to find a new location. Luckily, just up the hill at the end of Edge Street, the Municipal Water Works was vacating a large plot of land. In 1935, work began on the new Fox School buildings. These are the buildings we call home today.

The history of Fox is, in so many ways, the history of London. It unfurls in the poverty of Victorian London out of a desire by many, and in particular one determined woman, for a decent start for all children. Through the establishment of national school boards and the blossoming of Kensington and Chelsea with the expansion of the London underground, Fox is now home to the myriad of cultures and customs that make London so rich. And, reflecting Caroline Fox's family wishes, it nurtures children, no matter what their background. We hope she would be proud of how her little school has grown.

braised lamb shanks

Model and actress Liberty Ross, once a student at Fox, moved back to London after living in LA, when she was just seven. She had a very American accent and, at first, everyone teased her. "I soon made great friends who I am still friends with now." She says, "I remember tearing around the playground playing 'it'. I had such fun and my years at Fox were certainly some of the best years of my life!" This is her 'set and forget' dish. Get it ready early, pop it on the hob, and then lo and behold, as if by magic, dinner is ready! Serve with champ (an Irish dish of mashed potato and chopped spring onions) and green beans.

4	lamb shanks
	Seasoned flour
	Olive oil
1	tablespoon rosemary, chopped
½	tablespoon thyme, chopped
2	onions, red if you like, chopped
6	cloves of garlic, chopped
300	millilitres white wine
150	millilitres aged balsamic vinegar
2	slices orange peel and two bay leaves tied together with string

1 In a large ziplock bag combine seasoned flour and the lamb shanks. Shake until the lamb is coated then shake off any excess.

2 Heat 2 or 3 tablespoons of the olive oil in a heavy based saucepan and brown each shank quickly. Put them to one side.

3 Scrape up any burnt bits from the bottom of the pan. You might need to add a little more olive oil.

4 Heat the oil, add the rosemary and let it sizzle for a minute. Add the onions, thyme and garlic and fry gently until transparent but not brown.

5 Add the wine and balsamic and let it bubble furiously for a few minutes.

6 Add the lamb shanks and turn down the heat to a gentle simmer.

7 Tuck the orange peel and bay leaf in between the shanks.

8 Cover with a sheet of greaseproof paper, put the lid on top and simmer gently for about 2 hours, occasionally turning the shanks in the liquid.

9 They are cooked when the meat is almost falling off the bone (but only just!).

Note: Buy a good balsamic, not cheap, otherwise it won't taste as good. You can always use it afterwards in salads so it's a good investment.

SERVES 4

okra and lamb chops khoresht-e-bamiyeh

A 'Khoresht' is a Persian stew and Aida has given us this one from Abadan on the Iran/Iraq border. You can also make this with aubergine instead of okra if you prefer. It is best served with basmati rice to soak up the yummy juices. Leave out the lamb chops for a vegetarian or side dish.

450 grams fresh or frozen okra

450 grams lamb chops

6 cloves garlic

2 medium tomatoes, chopped

1 onion, chopped

3 tablespoons tomato purée

½ tablespoon turmeric powder

½ tablespoon mild curry powder

½ tablespoon ground black pepper

2 teaspoons fresh lemon juice

400 millilitres water

½ tablespoon saffron powder

1 big onion, finely chopped

4 teaspoons vegetable oil

1 Fry chopped onion in a large, non-stick pot until golden.

2 Add lamb chops to the pot and stir.

3 Add salt, pepper, curry powder, turmeric and saffron into the pot and stir the lamb chops until they become light brown (i.e. shallow-fried).

4 Add the peeled cloves of garlic, tomatoes and tomato purée and fry for 5 minutes.

5 Add the water, bring to the boil then turn the heat down and leave on a low heat until the sauce gets thick and meat becomes very tender (this may take up to 40 minutes).

6 Add the okra to the sauce and add another cup of water. Let it cook for another 20 minutes until the okra is cooked.

7 Add the lemon juice to the sauce at the end.

SERVES 4

diamond jubilee lamb, rosemary and red wine pie

Five generations of the Lidgate family have been Holland Park butchers for 160 years. During this time, they've served many generations of local residents, including Fox School families. Now they even supply the meat for Fox school dinners! This pie is a celebration of a fantastic national occasion, the Queen's Diamond Jubilee. They told us they were honoured to be involved with Fox Pot and to create an exclusive recipe using English ingredients that have been used in cooking for centuries. The making of the pastry crown turned out to be quite a challenge, but it was worth it in the end, with a photography session in the State Apartments at Kensington Palace.

1.3	kilograms diced leg organic English lamb
1	bottle red wine (Union Jack by Chapel Down or any good British wine)
2	onions, chopped
3	large carrots
800	grams chopped tomatoes
10	cloves fresh garlic, crushed
200	millilitres water
280	millilitres beef stock
3	tablespoons fresh rosemary, chopped
1	tablespoon fresh thyme, chopped
1	pinch sea salt to taste
500	grams puff pastry
	Olive oil
1	egg

1 Gently brown the lamb in olive oil for a few minutes.

2 Add the onions for a few minutes to slightly brown the carrots and garlic, sauté for a few minutes.

3 Deglaze with the wine, then add chopped tomatoes, beef stock and water. Bring to a simmer.

4 Add the thyme and rosemary and cover for approximately 1½–2 hours until lamb is tender.

5 When the stew has cooled, transfer it into a deep pie dish.

6 Dampen the edges of the dish with water. Roll out the pastry (5 millimetres thick and 5 centimetres larger than the dish size) and place it on top of the pie dish.

7 Seal pastry to edge and flute. Use the off-cuts to create decorations (leaves, flowers and of course a crown!).

8 Brush the surface with an egg wash.

9 Bake for 30 to 40 minutes at 220°C until golden brown.

SERVES 6

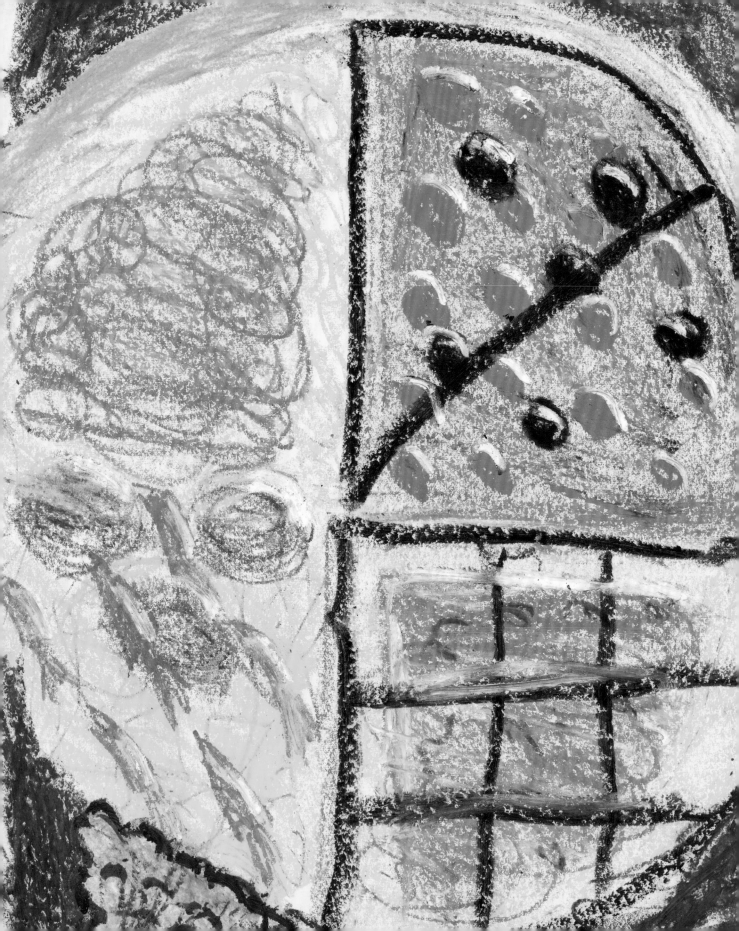

vegetarian

mr. cotter's veg loaf

This dish came about, as many great family dishes do, in response to the challenge of wildly different family appetites. In one corner, a daughter who had declared herself a committed vegetarian (at the age of four no less) and in the other our head teacher, a discerning meat eater. Paul took it upon himself to join her for a year, experimenting and testing all sorts of different dishes. By the end of that year she was longing for him to return to his meat-eating ways so that she no longer had to suffer his vegetarian experiments. This dish, however, has remained in the family repertoire. You can safely assume from the unforgiving palette of his tester that it's delicious!

2 cloves garlic

1 onion

1 courgette

A handful of mushrooms

1 tablespoon flour

1 egg

150 grams grated cheese

2 beef tomatoes

150 grams mixed chopped nuts

Red wine and Marmite to flavour

Butter

1 Chop the garlic, onion, courgette and mushrooms.

2 Fry onion and garlic before adding the mushrooms and courgettes.

3 When they have taken on some colour add the flour. Stir. Then add a splash of red wine to thicken and half a teaspoon of Marmite to taste.

4 Add the chopped tomatoes and the ground nuts, then add the egg. Mix and set aside.

5 Butter the dish or loaf tin. Spoon in half the mix before adding a layer of grated cheese. Spoon in the rest of the mix and top with a final sprinkling of cheese.

6 Bake in the oven for 25 to 35 minutes at 180°C.

7 It is best served warm the following day with fresh bread and a green salad.

SERVES 4 TO 5

aubergine parmigiana parmigiana di melanzane

Simona says this recipe is a MUST. Everybody in her hometown of Naples should be able to prepare it! You can serve as a starter or as a main and, if you want to make it slightly healthier, you could grill the aubergine instead of frying.

3	medium-sized aubergines
	Salt
	Extra virgin olive oil
	Basic tomato sauce
200	grams fresh mozzarella, thinly sliced
200	grams provola
½	cup freshly grated Parmigiano-Reggiano cheese
	A lot of basil

1 First prepare the tomato sauce. You can even make the sauce a couple of days before you want to make the parmigiana – just keep it well sealed in the fridge.

2 Preheat the oven to 200°C.

3 Wash and towel dry the aubergines. Slice them horizontally into 1-centimetre-thick circles.

4 Place the slices in a large colander, sprinkle with salt and set aside to rest about 30 minutes.

5 Drain and rinse the aubergine and dry on towels.

6 In a pan, heat the extra-virgin olive oil and fry the aubergine slices until light golden brown on both sides. Repeat with all of the pieces.

7 Take a small baking dish, then cover the base with a little of the tomato sauce and cover with a layer of aubergines, add some more tomato sauce.

8 Sprinkle with some pieces of mozzarella and provola, Parmigiano and basil leaves. Repeat the layers finishing with a layer of tomato sauce, parmesan and whole basil leaves.

9 Bake in the oven at 200°C for approximately 25 minutes. Allow to rest for a few minutes before cutting.

SERVES 6 TO 8

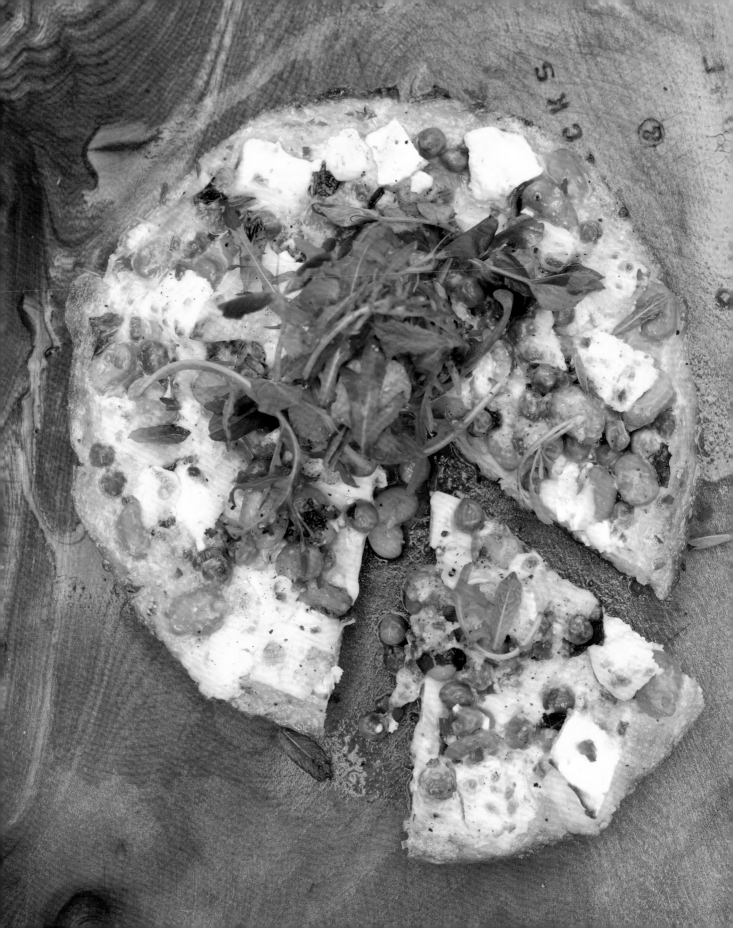

jamie oliver | england

summer veg and goat's cheese frittata

We are very excited to have Jamie's latest Recipease store and cooking school open at Notting Hill Gate, only two blocks from our school. Several Fox classes have had cooking lessons. We love Jamie Oliver's Kitchen Garden Project and all the other great work carried out by The Better Food Foundation. About his recipe, Jamie says, "You can think of this frittata as a posh omelette. It's delicious hot, but just as good cold so you can even try popping a wedge in your lunchbox."

A handful of fresh peas

A handful of fresh broad beans

1 fresh red chilli

6 large eggs, preferably free-range or organic

Sea salt and freshly ground black pepper

A few sprigs of fresh mint

A small knob of butter

Olive oil

1 lemon

65 grams goat's cheese

Parmesan cheese, for grating

1 Put a pan of salted water on to boil.

2 Shell your peas and broad beans by splitting open each pod lengthways and popping the peas and broad beans out into a bowl.

3 Blanch the peas and broad beans in the pan of boiling water for 30 seconds, then drain in a colander and leave to one side.

4 Halve, deseed and finely slice the chilli, then pick and roughly tear the mint leaves, discarding the stalks, and set aside.

5 Crack the eggs into a bowl with a pinch of pepper, then beat with a fork.

6 Preheat your grill to high. Melt a knob of butter in an ovenproof frying pan on a medium heat and when it sizzles, pour in the eggs.

7 Stir around gently with a spatula until you feel the egg start to set at the bottom, then straight away, turn the heat off so the frittata stays half cooked and quite runny.

8 In a bowl, toss the cooked peas, broad beans and mint in a splash of olive oil and a squeeze of lemon juice, then scatter them over the runny egg.

9 Break your goat's cheese into chunks and arrange over the top. Sprinkle over the sliced chilli and finely grate over some parmesan cheese.

10 Carefully place your frying pan under the grill for 2 to 3 minutes, or until the cheese is brown and bubbling and the frittata is cooked through.

SERVES 4

jollof rice

This is the West African version of the Spanish Paella, the Indian Biriyani and the Cajun Jambalaya. It goes wonderfully with dodo (fried plantain) but you can also add chicken, fish, ham or goat! Feel free to experiment and come up with your own family's version of this rice dish.

¼ cup oil

5 cups water or stock

2 onions, chopped

1 red or green bell pepper, chopped

3–4 cloves garlic, minced

3 cups long grain rice

¼ cup tomatoes, chopped

2 carrots, peeled and chopped

1 cup green beans

1 cup cabbage, chopped

Salt and pepper to taste

1 Heat the oil over a medium flame. Add the onions and peppers, sauté until the onions are wilted and translucent, 4 to 5 minutes.

2 Add the garlic and sauté for another 1 to 2 minutes.

3 Stir the rice into the onions and peppers and heat through for another 1 to 2 minutes.

4 Stir in the tomato paste to coat the rice and give it a reddish hue.

5 Add the chopped tomatoes and let them cook down for 2 to 3 minutes.

6 Add the carrots, green beans and cabbage. Season well with salt and pepper.

7 Bring to the boil, then reduce heat to low, cover tightly and simmer for 20 minutes.

8 Remove from heat, leave to rest for another 10 minutes.

SERVES 4 TO 6

pasta a la norma

This recipe was named after Vincenzo Bellini's most famous opera, 'La Norma'. Apparently, the Sicilian composer loved this pasta and like Simona, we couldn't agree more. This recipe is one of Simona's favourites, not least because it evokes wonderful memories of her childhood holidays spent in Sicily with her nonna. "Try your best to find ricotta salata," says Simona, "it really makes all the difference."

2   medium aubergine, thinly sliced

1   small red onion, chopped

1   handful fresh basil

5–6   big plum tomatoes or 800 grams cherry tomatoes or even a good italian passata

100   grams ricotta salata (or pecorino if not available)

500   grams spaghetti or penne pasta

  Extra virgin olive oil

  Salt and pepper

  Chilli (optional)

1 Sprinkle the sliced aubergines with salt and put them in colander for an hour to remove any bitterness. Place the slices on paper towels to drain.

2 Heat the olive oil in a large skillet and brown the aubergines on both sides.

3 If you are using plum tomatoes remove the skin by immersing them for a minute in boiling water and then peeling them. There is no need if you are using cherry tomatoes.

4 Heat some olive oil and fry the chopped onion. When it starts to colour add the chopped tomatoes or passata, salt and pepper, and chilli if you are using it. Leave to cook for 15 minutes.

5 In the meantime cook the pasta 'al dente' as per the pack instructions.

6 When the pasta is ready, drain it and place it in the pan with the sauce.

7 Mix everything together. Add some leaves of fresh basil, the grated ricotta salata , some olive oil and half the aubergine slices.

8 Serve the pasta in dishes, topped with the remaining aubergine slices, some more grated ricotta salata, a bit of olive oil, fresh basil leaves and if you're lucky, a little Sicilian sunshine.

SERVES 4

ricotta and lemon ravioli with butter and fresh mint ravioli ripieni di ricotta e limone con salsa di burro e menta

Legendary Italian chef, Gennaro, was given this recipe by Antonio, the local pasta-maker in his home village, Minori, on the Amalfi Coast. When he made this in England, he found that he had to keep adding more lemon zest and juice because the lemons he'd been using in Italy were so much more pungent. When you make the filling, taste it and if necessary add more lemon – but only the zest or the filling will become mushy. This just makes you want to stretch out in a hammock among the lemon groves, doesn't it?

FOR THE PASTA

200 grams '00' flour

2 medium eggs

FOR THE FILLING

225 grams ricotta

4 tablespoons lemon zest

2 teaspoons lemon juice

2 tablespoons parmesan cheese, freshly grated

Salt to taste

FOR THE SAUCE

100 grams butter

30 mint leaves

4 teaspoons lemon juice

4 tablespoons parmesan cheese, freshly grated

PASTA DOUGH

1 Place the flour into a large bowl or on a clean work surface. Make a well in the centre and break in the eggs.

2 With a fork or your hands gradually mix the flour with the eggs, then knead with your hands for about 5 minutes until you get a smooth dough; it should be pliable but not sticky.

3 Shape the dough into a ball, wrap in cling film and leave for about 30 minutes.

FILLING

1 Place the ricotta in a bowl and squash with a fork.

2 Mix in the lemon zest, lemon juice, parmesan cheese and salt and mix together well.

3 With the help of two tablespoons, form the mixture into small balls about 2 centimetres in diameter and set aside.

ASSEMBLING

1 Divide the pasta dough into 4 portions and use it one piece at a time keeping the rest wrapped in cling film so it doesn't dry out.

2 Roll the pasta out in a pasta machine or use a rolling pin to roll out into a paper-thin rectangle. Lay the pasta sheet on a lightly floured work surface with a short edge nearest to you.

3 Put balls of the filling in a line down the pasta sheet about ¾ of the way in from one side, spacing them about 2.5 centimetres apart.

4 Fold the sheet lengthways in half and press with your fingertips between the balls of filling to seal.

5 Cut the filling with a ravioli wheel or a sharp knife.

6 Gather up all the trimmings, re-roll and repeat. It's important to work quite quickly, so the pasta doesn't dry out. When you have finished, repeat with the remaining pieces of dough.

SAUCE

1 Meanwhile melt the butter in a frying pan together with the fresh mint leaves.

2 Add the lemon juice and cook on a gentle heat until the butter begins to bubble.

COOKING

1 Bring a large saucepan of slightly salted water to the boil, drop in the ravioli and cook for about 3 minutes until 'al dente'.

2 Quickly drain the ravioli, reserving a couple of tablespoons of the cooking water.

3 Add the cooked ravioli to the sauce together with a couple of tablespoons of the pasta water to help give it a little more moisture.

4 Add the parmesan cheese and serve immediately with some grated lemon zest and a sprig of fresh mint.

SERVES 4

singapore fried vermicelli

Valerie's fried vermicelli are one of the favourites from International Evening and the Fox Summer Fair Café. Cooked in a big deep wok-like pan called a Kwali, it's a dish that Singaporean kids grow up with, always dished out from a big pot at parties or picnics. In Singapore, the vegetarian version is very common in hawker centres all over the island. Although it can be found at any time of the day, it is actually a breakfast favourite. You can easily add chicken or any other type of meat to this dish if preferred.

3 packets rice vermicelli

2 packets bean sprouts

1 Chinese cabbage

3 onions

10 carrots

3 packets green leaves like choi sum

8 eggs

2 spring onions

2 cubes vegetable stock

Oil for frying

Soya sauce to taste

Pepper to taste

1 Soak vermicelli in hot water until soft then drain the water.

2 Remove roots of bean sprouts, rinse and set aside.

3 Cut Chinese cabbage, onions, carrots, choi sum and spring onions into strips.

4 Prepare vegetable stock and set aside.

5 Fry eggs and cut into strips and set this also to one side.

6 Fry onions, Chinese cabbage, choi sum, bean sprouts and carrots.

7 Add vermicelli and vegetable stock.

8 Stir until all ingredients are well mixed.

9 Add soya sauce and pepper, to taste.

10 Garnish with strips of eggs and spring onions.

Note: Rice vermicelli such as Yeo's, 375 grams per packet, can be purchased at Asian supermarkets like the one on Queensway.

SERVES 50 TASTING PORTIONS

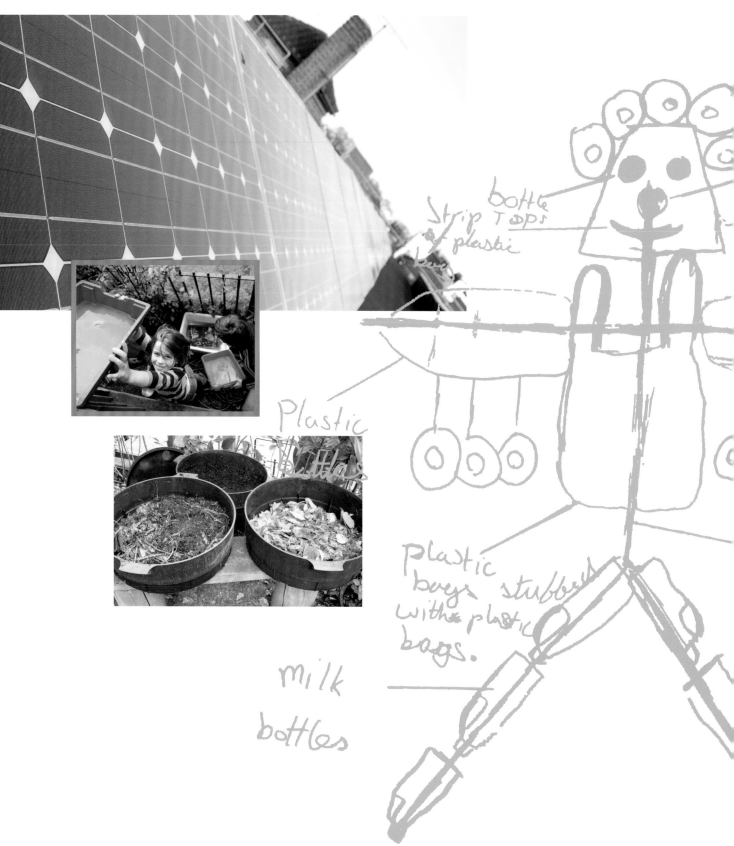

bottle
strip Tops
of plastic

Plastic
bottles

Plastic
bags stuffed
with plastic
bags.

milk
bottles

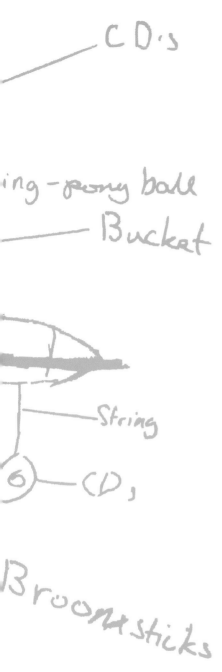

CD's

ing - pong ball

Bucket

String

CD,

Broomsticks

We might be giving you the impression that at Fox School all we care about is food. Not so! In the summer of 2012 Fox Primary School was very proud to receive the Green Flag Award. This is the highest award a school can be given by Eco-Schools, the International Award Programme that guides schools on their journey to sustainability. This is more than just a process, more than just box-ticking. At its heart, it means that everyone at Fox – the teachers, parents and children – is determined to make the environment and, in particular, sustainability a priority, by including it across the whole curriculum and in the very fabric of school life.

green fox

Fox is the first school in the Royal Borough of Kensington and Chelsea to receive this award. When the Eco-Schools assessment team visited the school they were amazed at the commitment and knowledge demonstrated by the children of the Fox eco committee who were grilled for over an hour! And some of the questions were tough. The children answered knowledgeably and honestly – sometimes a little too honestly (we might have preferred that they didn't mention how they'd caught out Ms. Waddell for leaving her computer turned on when she wasn't using it!).

But the assessment team was more than satisfied. They loved the very visible recycling efforts as well as the use of water butts, reflective film on the windows, and solar panels. Who wouldn't be amazed by the solar panels? Fox is the first school in London to have them and the solar surface is the second largest in London. But it was the extent to which the children understood their mission and were leading the eco journey that made the assessment team wholeheartedly recommend Fox for a Green Flag award.

roasted bell peppers stuffed with quinoa

The Fox Pot has been lucky to receive support from many different corners of our community. The people at Whole Foods Market, in particular, have been excited about the Fox Pot cookbook from the start. Committed as they are to foods that are fresh, wholesome and taste wonderful, free of preservatives, colours, flavours, sweeteners and hydrogenated fats, they jumped at the chance to share a favourite recipe with the Fox Pot. There will be looks of envy from the meat-eating crowd when you serve this colourful and delicious entrée of bell peppers stuffed with mushrooms, carrots, spinach, quinoa and cashews.

1	tablespoon olive oil, plus more for oiling the pan
1	red onion, chopped
225	grams sliced mushrooms
1	cup chopped carrots
7	bell peppers (1 cored, seeded and chopped; tops removed and reserved from remaining six then cored and seeded)
½	cup chopped parsley
115	grams baby spinach
1½	teaspoon ground cinnamon
¾	teaspoon ground cumin
1	cup uncooked quinoa, rinsed and cooked according to package directions
	Salt and pepper to taste
½	cup roasted, salted cashews

1 Heat oil in a large skillet over medium high heat. Add onion and cook, stirring occasionally until transparent, 8 to 10 minutes.

2 Add mushrooms and cook until softened, 4 to 5 minutes more. Add carrots and chopped peppers, cook until just softened, then add parsley and spinach (in batches, if needed). Let spinach wilt then stir in cinnamon, cumin and cooked quinoa. Toss gently to combine.

3 Add salt, pepper and cashews and cook 1 to 2 minutes more. Set aside to let filling cool until just warm.

4 Meanwhile, preheat oven to 180°c. Grease a 20 x 30 centimetre baking pan with oil and set aside.

5 Divide quinoa mixture evenly among remaining six bell peppers, gently packing it down and making sure to fully fill each pepper. Top each pepper with its reserved top then arrange them upright in prepared pan.

6 Cover snugly with foil and bake, checking halfway through, until peppers are tender and juicy and filling is hot throughout, about an hour.

7 Transfer to plates and serve.

SERVES 6

cauliflower and potato curry

Shaun is one of our wonderful teaching assistants. He was also the main mo-ver and shaker behind the school's contribution to 'Mo-vember'. This curry is all about indulgence so serve it with a lovely big dollop of Greek-style yoghurt (or plain cottage cheese if you prefer). Shaun's top tip is to avoid stirring the curry while cooking as the vegetables (especially cauliflower) will start losing their structure; it's nice if they can remain as whole as possible. Serve with fresh, whole-wheat roti, paratha or naan bread of your choice; or with basmati rice. Once cooked, add extra chopped tomatoes, a large handful of fresh coriander for vibrancy and a chilli for heat (an optional extra for the brave).

1	whole cauliflower
3	potatoes
3	tomatoes
1	white onion
50	grams frozen or fresh peas
1	carrot
300	millilitres water
2	tablespoons vegetable or sunflower oil
1	teaspoon whole cumin seeds
1	green chilli seeded and diced
	A handful fresh coriander, chopped (for garnish)

FOR THE SPICE MIX

1	teaspoon tomato purée
½	teaspoon fresh ginger, grated
½	teaspoon turmeric powder
2	teaspoons salt to taste
½	teaspoon red chilli (optional)
1	teaspoon ground cumin

1 Peel potatoes (or leave skins on if preferred) and carrot.

2 Cut cauliflower into medium-sized florets.

3 Dice potatoes and tomatoes into 2-centimetre chunks.

4 Chop onion finely.

5 Heat oil in a medium-to large-sized, heavy pan on medium heat.

6 Add cumin seeds and fry until golden.

7 Add onion and cook until golden brown.

8 Add the whole spice mix and cook until golden.

9 Add potatoes, carrots and stir occasionally for 5 minutes.

10 Add cauliflower and peas. Gently stir.

11 Add water and cover with lid allowing it to cook for 20 to 25 minutes until soft.

SERVES 4 TO 6

JAM

sides

irish wheaten bread

Susan is half Irish and grew up with soda or wheaten bread or brown scones baked almost daily by her mother who was following in the tradition of generations of Irish women. Now Susan's husband and children absolutely love wheaten bread, so the tradition continues. Whole Foods Market is the easiest place in West London to buy the flours you need, although you can buy wonderful wholemeal flour and oats online from companies such as Pimhill, albeit in semi-industrial quantities. The bread, with vitamin B, is much healthier than white bread. It is really delicious straight out of the oven, slightly warm with salted butter. You can serve it with honey, jam or smoked salmon.

550	grams coarse wholemeal flour (not strong wholemeal flour)
350	grams plain (all purpose) flour
100	grams brown flour
1½	teaspoons salt
2	teaspoons bicarbonate of soda
½	teaspoon cream of tartar
6	tablespoons jumbo oats
½	a beaten egg
2	tablespoons honey
1	tablespoon olive oil
25	grams butter, melted
770	millilitres buttermilk

1 Preheat the oven to 200°C. Grease 2 or 3 1-kilogram loaf tins.

2 Sieve all the dry ingredients except the oats together, and then stir in the oats. Mix the wet ingredients together in a bowl or jug. If the honey is not runny, stir this mixture until you have got most of the lumps out.

3 Spoon the bread mixture into tins. Very gently smooth the tops so there aren't lumps or spikes. Don't press it down or you will make the bread heavy. Pop the tins in the oven for about 1 to 1½ hours to if you have two loaves and about 50 minutes if you have three loaves. If they are cooking too fast on top, turn the oven down to 180°C.

4 When you take them out of the oven, turn them out of the tins and let them cool on a rack.

SERVES 8

crispy seaweed

This is one of Will's recipes that attempts to 'sneak' vitamins into his children (the other one is an avocado shake found in the 'Treats' section). His kids, like most, really like crispy seaweed from the local Chinese restaurant, which is essentially deep fried cabbage with sugar, something that's not very good for you, but tastes very nice. This version, by contrast, is both very good for you and very delicious.

1 bag curly kale from the supermarket.

2 tablespoons oil of your choice.

1 flavouring of your choice (salt or soya, teriyaki, bit of a stock cube etc)

1 tablespoon of sweetness (icing sugar or caster sugar)

1 Mix the kale with the oil. Oils with flavour work well.

2 Splash in your flavour of choice but be careful not to make the kale wet as it will take much longer to dry and go crispy.

3 Sprinkle the sugar onto the cabbage and mix. The sugar caramelises and helps the kale go crispy.

4 Put in the oven on a baking sheet at around 180°C for 30 minutes. Job done, crispy seaweed.

Note: Depending on the oven and how much 'wet' you put on the kale, it can take a little longer to go crispy. Check on the kale and move it about the pan a bit every 15 minutes or so. You can also cook it slow and perfect at 100°C for about an hour; just keep checking on it and give it a mix, until it is all crispy, yummy, delicious.

SERVES 4

vegetable chutney achar

This is a fresh chutney and is an essential part of Malay weddings. The vinegar helps the vegetables keep well without going soggy – this is pretty important for Malay weddings since they run over the course of a weekend with guests coming and going, eating constantly!

200 grams carrots, thinly sliced

200 grams cucumbers, thinly sliced

200 grams fine beans, cut in inch pieces

1 teaspoon mustard seeds

½ teaspoon turmeric powder

¼ cup white vinegar

Salt and sugar to taste

A thumb-sized piece ginger, thinly sliced

3 garlic cloves

1 Heat oil in a wok until smoking. Put in mustard seeds, garlic cloves (whole) and ginger. Cook for about a minute.

2 Mix the rest of the ingredients in the wok. Quickly stir for a minute and turn off the heat.

SERVES 4 TO 6

coconut rice with anchovy sambal
nasi lemak with ikan bilis

This is a very common street food in South East Asia, unofficially considered Malaysia's national dish, though the Indonesians might not agree. It is sold everywhere, from roadside stalls to school canteens and even high-end restaurants. Every child has it etched in their childhood memories. Although it is a breakfast favourite, it can be eaten any time of day. Traditionally, in old Malaysia kampungs (villages), it was wrapped in banana leaves and newspaper and sold to labourers for lunch.

FOR THE COCONUT RICE

5	cups basmati rice
1	tablespoon salt
2	pandan leaves
	A thumb-size piece ginger, sliced
200	millilitres coconut milk
5	cups water

FOR THE ANCHOVY SAMBAL

100	grams small dried anchovies
3	tablespoons ground chilli paste or chilli powder
1	large white onion sliced
1	tablespoon tamarind sauce
	Salt and sugar to taste
	Vegetable oil
	A cup of water

COCONUT RICE

1 Wash rice several times in cold water and drain.

2 Mix all ingredients in a rice cooker. If you do not have a rice cooker, put the ingredients in a saucepan and bring to the boil, then reduce the heat, put the lid on and leave for 15 to 20 minutes.

4 Once cooked, fluff the rice and leave to cool.

ANCHOVY SAMBAL

1 Fry anchovies in oil until brown/crispy and drain.

2 Heat oil in a wok and put in the ground chilli paste (or powder) together with 1 cup of water for 10 minutes.

3 Mix the tamarind sauce, salt and sugar into the wok and stir.

4 Mix in the fried anchovies and sliced onions.

SERVES 6 TO 8

cornmeal arepas

These are one of the national dishes of Venezuela where there are many food stands called areperas that sell them. They are a corn pancake of sorts. Angela says you can split them like a bagel or pita bread and then fill with ham, cheese or whatever you like. They are best eaten warm. The cornmeal used to make arepas is a special, pre-cooked variety that usually goes by the name masarepa, or masa precocida. It can be found in Latin American food shops.

210	grams cornmeal flour
1	teaspoon salt
310	millilitres water

1 Mix all ingredients together and knead the dough until well blended (approximately 5 minutes).

2 Take small amounts of dough and form balls.

3 Pat them to form a shape and size similar to a crumpet.

4 Place a little bit of oil in a frying pan and cook until golden on each side.

SERVES 4

spiced tomato relish

Nina is the fabulous Fox Head Chef. She is in charge of all the healthy, delicious dinners served every day to Fox children. We don't know how she does it. This chutney sells like hot cakes at the school fair and is lovely served with cheese in a sandwich or as a sauce for burgers or hotdogs.

2	kilograms ripe tomatoes
450	grams onions, chopped
2	cloves garlic, crushed
5	centimetres fresh ginger, peeled and grated
6	fresh red chillies, de-seeded and finely chopped or 1 teaspoon cayenne powder
340	grams dark brown sugar
290	millilitres malt vinegar
110	grams sultanas
2	teaspoons sea salt
1	teaspoon mustard seeds
1	teaspoon coriander seeds

1 Place tomatoes in boiling water for 20 seconds, then plunge them into cold water. Use a knife to peel away the skins.

2 Coarsely chop tomatoes and place in a large saucepan.

3 Add the remaining ingredients and bring to the boil, stirring constantly.

4 Reduce the heat to a simmer.

5 Cook for about 2 hours or until the chutney is thick and syrupy.

6 Ladle into sterilised jars and seal.

7 Store in a cool, dark place for 1 month before using.

SERVES MANY

barbara bird's runner bean chutney

Miss Bird, one of our superb year one teachers, told us, "My parents came to visit last summer and left me with a few huge bags of runner beans from their garden. Unsure what to do with them, I phoned my nan. Fifteen minutes later, she was reciting the recipe down the phone (whilst I tried to google the conversions from pounds to grams.) This recipe is a firm family favourite now and great with some nice strong cheddar and fresh bread – at least that's how I like it."

1	kilogram runner beans, sliced (use a bean slicer)
700	grams onions, chopped
850	millilitres malt vinegar
50	grams cornflour
1	tablespoon mustard powder (normal mustard is fine, just be a little more generous)
1	tablespoon turmeric
250	grams soft brown sugar
450	grams Demerara sugar
6	500-gram jars

1 Put the chopped onions and 280 millilitre of the vinegar into a casserole pan. Simmer for 20 minutes, or until soft.

2 Meanwhile, cook beans in salted water for 10 minutes, then strain and add to the onions.

3 Mix the cornflour, mustard and turmeric with a little of the vinegar to form a paste.

4 Add the paste to the onion mixture and pour in the rest of the vinegar. Simmer for 10 minutes, then stir in the sugar until dissolved and simmer for a further 15 minutes.

5 Put into warm sterilised jars, cover with cling film and lids. Leave the jars for one month before eating.

Tip: Sterilise your jars in a clean bowl of boiling water, then carefully remove them with tongs and dry them in a warm oven. This will keep them super clean and still warm. Don't worry about spending a fortune on jar toppers, just use a bit of cling film in between the jar and the lid.

MAKES 6 JARS

smoked mackerel pâté

Poppy explained to us that this unlikely family favourite snuck into the household recipe book when the children were small, before they thought they didn't like fish. At the time, Marielle, a French friend, explained that she had gone to see her doctor in France with her four year old who was not really enjoying his food. "Has he had Roquefort yet?" asked the doctor. "No," she replied. "Is it good for his tummy?" "No, no, it's for his palate." On her advice, Poppy tried to educate her children's palates and this is one of Marielle's recipes. Of course, if your child's culinary horizons are not (yet) so wide, you can always finish it all yourself.

300 grams skinless smoked mackerel

½ pot Greek yoghurt

1 teaspoon French mustard

Splash of cream

1 Flake the mackerel fillets in a bowl with two spoons.

2 Add the yoghurt and mustard.

3 Mix together.

4 Add a splash of cream for extra sweetness.

5 Serve with a warm baguette and some butter.

SERVES 4

onion squash purée with roasted chestnuts
purée de potimarron aux chataîgnes

Florence enjoyed growing this once forgotten ancient vegetable in her mother's country garden near Barbizon, the painters' village. The name in French: "potimarron" is a combination of "potiron" (pumpkin) and "marron" (chestnut). Its rich chestnutty/carrot flavour and the fact that it can be stored all winter long make it a perfect vegetable for the chilly season. This dish brings comfort and warmth as the ideal companion to game, poultry and fish.

2 kilograms onion squash

350 grams whole chestnuts (in jar, tin or vacuum-packed)

A knob of butter

1 large tablespoon goose fat (or duck fat)

Salt

Fresh ground pepper

Nutmeg (optional)

1 tablespoon crème fraîche (optional)

1 Put a large pot of salted water on to boil.

2 Cut both ends of the onion squash, then cut it in half.

3 Spoon out the seeds and cut both halves in segments. Use a strong knife as the onion squash's flesh is very hard.

4 Remove the skin with a vegetable peeler.

5 Cut the onion squash in medium cubes.

6 Put the cubes in the boiling water and boil them until cooked (they should be crumbly but not soggy).

7 Strain the cooked onion squash.

8 In a medium saucepan, on medium heat, melt the goose fat and, when sizzling, add the chestnuts, season and stir until roasted. Reserve three for decoration.

9 In the pot, add a knob of butter and whisk the onion squash until smooth and hot. Add some crème fraîche for extra creaminess. Season with salt, pepper and nutmeg.

10 Add the roasted chestnuts to the puréed onion squash. Decorate by placing three chestnuts in the centre.

Variation: Mix 150 grams of grated gruyère cheese to the puréed onion squash (with or without the chestnuts). Place mixture in an oven-proof dish. Sprinkle with grated gruyère and a few little cubes of butter. Brown under a hot grill until golden.

SERVES 6

11/2012 Lo N327
Bonne
AIOLI
Mama

habibi

desserts

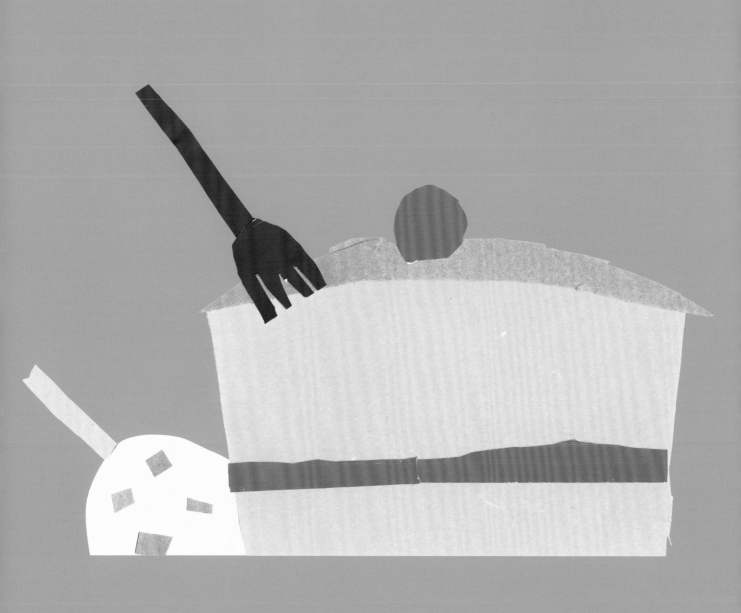

cakes

chocolate almond cake

Author and Fox mum, Isabel Wolff, contributed this kid-tested recipe. Her children, Alice and Eddie, love helping to make this cake. Their Austrian grandmother, Eva, has made it for over 60 years. It would be lovely served with a dollop of whipped cream or crème fraîche and either some raspberries or cherries. While it's cooking, it's okay to check on the cake as it's tolerant and will not sink. Once it's started to come away from the sides of the tin, and the skewer comes out clean, then it's ready. Keep checking and consider turning the oven down for the last 10 minutes or so. This cake, having no flour, is gluten-free.

250 grams dark chocolate (Bournville works well)

125 grams caster sugar

175 grams unsalted butter

200 grams almonds, ground

4 eggs, separated, the whites whisked to stiff peaks

5 teaspoons apricot conserve, to glaze

50 grams icing sugar

3–4 glacé cherries to decorate

1 Butter the sides of a 25-centimetre cake tin. Preheat oven to 170°C.

2 Melt 175 grams of the chocolate in a bowl over a pan of boiling water. Remove from heat.

3 In a large bowl, cream 125 grams of the butter with all of the sugar.

4 Add the separated egg yolks.

5 Add the ground almonds and stir again.

6 Add the melted chocolate and stir again.

7 Fold in the whisked egg whites.

8 Pour this mixture into the prepared tin and cook on 170°C for 30 to 40 minutes.

9 Turn out onto a cake rack.

10 When cool, coat with a glaze of apricot conserve.

11 Melt the remaining 75 grams of chocolate with the remaining 50 grams of butter. Stir in the icing sugar.

12 Ice the cake liberally and decorate with a few glacé cherries.

Tip: When we were testing this recipe we melted the chocolate in the microwave. This works fine as long as you take it slowly, on a low power and keep checking and stirring at least every minute.

SERVES 8

grandma's date and banana bread

Scott's grandma lives in Norfolk and he says that she's a really good cook! This is a lovely morning teacake. Spread a little butter on a nice thick slice while it's still warm – sublime. When this was cooked for the photograph, we could hardly concentrate for the smell. You've never seen photos taken so quickly. Needless to say we devoured the lot.

250 grams dried dates, pitted

90 millilitres water

1 lemon, zest and juice

2 ripe bananas

175 grams unsalted butter, softened

175 grams caster sugar

3 eggs

225 grams self-raising white flour

½ teaspoon baking powder

½ teaspoon ground cinnamon (optional)

1 Grease and line a 1.2-litre loaf tin.

2 Set aside four dates. Place the rest in a small, heavy-based saucepan with the water and lemon zest. Bring to the boil, reduce heat and simmer gently for five minutes until the dates are soft and pulpy.

3 Purée the mixture in a food processor until smooth or mash together in a bowl using a fork.

4 Mash the bananas until smooth.

5 Cream the butter and sugar together in a bowl until pale and fluffy.

6 Add the banana purée and eggs to the creamed butter and sugar.

7 Sift the flour, baking powder and cinnamon into the bowl and beat until thoroughly combined.

8 Spoon a third of the banana mixture into the prepared loaf tin and level the surface.

9 Spread half of the date purée over the surface. Repeat these layers once, then cover with the remaining banana mixture.

10 Cut the reserved dates into slivers and scatter over the surface.

11 Bake at 160°c for 1 to 1¼ hours until well risen and firm.

12 Leave in the tin for 15 minutes, then transfer to a wire rack to cool.

13 Store in an airtight container for up to a week.

SERVES 6 TO 8

strawberry cake

Rowley, restaurateur and one of the leading lights of modern British cooking is also a former Fox parent. He gave us this recipe which he said was a pleasant way of spending an afternoon. Rowley recommends a sticky white wine, such as Sauternes, to go with strawberries. Though, for him, a few plain strawberries, bereft of cream and sugar, but with a glass of Beaujolais-Villages in which to dip them from time to time is perfection.

FOR THE SPONGE

4	eggs
125	grams caster sugar
125	grams flour
1	lemon, zest only
30	grams butter

FOR THE PASTRY CREAM

¼	litre milk
50	grams caster sugar
2	egg yolks
30	grams flour
1	vanilla pod
	Icing sugar

ASSEMBLING THE CAKE

500	grams large strawberries
150	millilitres whipping cream
3	tablespoons Grand Marnier or Curaçao
100	grams caster sugar
125	grams marzipan
	Green food colouring

THE SPONGE

1 Preheat the oven to 180°C. Butter and flour a 23-centimetre cake tin.

2 Melt the butter in a small pan (or microwave).

3 Combine the eggs and sugar in a mixing bowl and place over a large pan of boiling water. Whisking sporadically, heat the mixture until a little warmer than blood heat.

4 Remove the bowl from bain-marie and whisk the mixture constantly and vigorously, either in an electric mixer, with an electric hand-held whisk or with an old fashioned mechanical whisk (surprisingly effective, and minimises washing up). Continue until the mixture becomes very pale, has increased greatly in volume and is a thick mayonnaise-like texture.

5 Fold in the lemon zest at this point.

6 Sieve the flour onto a sheet of greaseproof paper and then, very slowly, start to pour it into the egg and sugar mixture.

7 Continue to fold it in very gently, little by little so that the flour is absorbed without losing too much air in the process. Take care that no flour settles on the bottom of the bowl.

8 When the mixture is completely mixed, slowly pour in the tepid melted butter. Fold it in equally gently, then pour this cake batter into the cake tin.

9 Bake for 30 minutes. The cake will be cooked when it is puffed up, a good golden brown, and springs back to the touch. Turn out onto a cake rack and cool.

THE PASTRY CREAM

1 Split the vanilla pod and scrape out some of the seeds into the milk in a saucepan. Bring them to the boil and leave to infuse for twenty minutes.

2 Whisk together the egg yolks and sugar in a bowl and, when well mixed, blend in the flour (add a few drops of milk if the mixture is too thick).

3 Bring the milk back to the boil and then pour into the mixture, whisking constantly.

4 Return the mixture to the saucepan and bring back to the boil, still whisking constantly.

5 Let the mixture simmer for a couple of minutes, still whisking, and then pour into a small bowl.

6 Dust the surface with a little icing sugar and leave to cool.

TO ASSEMBLE

1 Dissolve the sugar in four tablespoons of water, heating it gently to make a little syrup. Add two tablespoons of the liqueur to this.

2 Whip the cream until quite stiff. Remove the vanilla pod from the pastry cream and whisk in the remaining tablespoon of liqueur. Apart from flavouring, this will help the mixture to become a little smoother and less thick.

3 Fold in the cream until beautifully smooth, light but quite rich.

4 With a long bread knife, split the sponge in two equal halves to produce two cakes. Lay the bottom layer base-side down in the cake tin.

5 Brush the exposed, cut surface copiously with half the syrup.

6 Spoon in a small amount of the pastry cream, forcing it down in the gap where the cake has shrunk from the sides of the tin.

7 Cut the best strawberries in half and arrange them, upside down, around the outside circumference of the cake so that the cut sides touch the outside, producing a kind of wall of strawberries around the middle of the cake.

8 Cut the remainder of the strawberries into quarters and mix them with the cream mixture. Fill the middle of the cake with this cream, pushing it to the outside so that the 'wall' is held in place. Level off the surface with a spatula.

9 Soak the remaining half of the sponge with the rest of the syrup and lay on top of the cream, cut side uppermost. Push the sponge gently down, making sure it is perfectly flat so that the cream starts to fill the gap between the cake and the tin. Refrigerate the cake for two hours.

10 Work the marzipan on a board, adding a few drops of the food colouring. Continue to work it with your hands until it has formed a soft malleable mass and the colour is a uniform pale green.

11 Dust the board or a marble and roll out the marzipan into a disc very slightly larger than the cake.

12 Very carefully, invert a large serving plate over the cake in its tin and turn the cake over. Lift the tin off the assembled cake, giving it a little turn if it proves at all stubborn.

13 Place the marzipan disc over the top of the cake and trim it to fit with a very sharp knife.

14 Place a whole strawberry that you have cunningly reserved for the purpose on top and serve.

SERVES 6 TO 8

SUN EXCLUSIVE

The winner of our raffle for bath oil and soap is ..The Queen!

A RAFFLE prize of two bars of soap and bath oil has been won by THE QUEEN.

Organisers couldn't believe it when a winning ticket was pulled out with "The Queen, Buckingham Palace" written on it.

A prankster was suspected and the stub was about to be thrown away, with a redraw for the £10 prize. But a fellow punter in the summer raffle at Fox Primary School in Notting Hill, West London, revealed that the ticket WAS genuine.

A courtier at Buckingham Palace has children at the school – and the Queen offered to buy some tickets after overhearing him selling them to other workers.

Her name then went into the hat with thousands of others.

A source said: "I understand Her Majesty has been formally notified about her lucky win, but has not yet come to claim her prize."

One parent said: "I enter this raffle every year and I've never won anything. It's amazing that she won."

The Queen is known to prefer a bath to a shower. In 2001 The Sun revealed that she plays with a rubber duck at bathtime.

A source at Buckingham Palace said: "This is not the first time The Queen has taken part in raffles. Like most people she thinks they are a bit

By DUNCAN LARCOMBE
Royal Correspondent

of fun and a great way to raise money. I have no idea whether she has ever been lucky enough to win a prize before but the fact that she has won bath oil is very amusing.

"She loves to relax in the bath and I am sure she will be looking forward to getting her hands on her windfall."

● THE Queen is Europe's second wealthiest monarch with a £1.2billion fortune – £800million less than Prince Hans-Adam, ruler of tax haven Liechtenstein, a Belgian rich list reveals.

d.larcombe@the-sun.co.uk

The Sun Says — Page Eight

QUEEN HAS RUBBER DUCK IN HER BATH
...and it wears a crown!

Order of bath . . . Sun story of Queen and duck

In amongst Gloria's boxes of Fox photos and memorabilia we found this article from 2007 – proof that the hands into which Fox raffle tickets pass are many and varied!

traditional irish christmas cake

Another cake from a grandmother, but where else would you expect a traditional Christmas cake to come from? Nadia and Gregory make around six of this, their grandmother's adaptation of a rich fruit cake, every year as they make terrific gifts. Joanne, their Mum, tells us they never ice them, as everyone in their family tends to pick off the icing! Their grandmother soaks the fruit the night before in brandy, but sherry, port or whiskey would do. The fruit soaks up the alcohol and takes on a wonderful aroma. Make sure you have a big bowl and a strong wooden spoon – and a bit of elbow grease, it can be quite tough work!

230 grams plain flour

1 teaspoon mixed spice

1 teaspoon cinnamon

1 teaspoon grated nutmeg

1 teaspoon cocoa powder

170 grams butter

170 grams soft brown sugar

1 tablespoon black treacle

1 teaspoon each orange and lemon peel, finely-grated

4 eggs

575 grams mixed dried fruit (currants, sultanas and seedless raisins)

115 grams chopped mixed peel or dried cranberries

60 grams walnut halves or blanched almonds, chopped

60 grams dates, chopped

60 grams glacé cherries, chopped

2 tablespoons milk

1 Brush a 20-centimetre round tin with melted butter. Sprinkle with flour and shake tin to make sure all the butter is covered with a fine layer of flour.

2 Sift flour with spice, cinnamon, grated nutmeg and cocoa.

3 Cream butter with sugar, treacle, lemon and orange peel.

4 Beat in whole eggs, one at a time, adding a tablespoon of sifted dry ingredients with each.

5 Stir in dates and cherries.

6 Fold in dry ingredients and smooth top with knife.

7 Bake in centre of cool oven at 140°c for about 4 hours (or until a fine knitting needle inserted into centre of cake comes out clean).

8 Leave in tin for 15 minutes before turning out onto wire cooling rack.

9 When completely cold, wrap in aluminium foil and store in airtight tin until needed.

Note: this cake will keep for up to three months, and is probably at its best about 4 weeks after baking.

Tip: to avoid having clumps of cherries in the cake, slice them in half and roll them in flour before adding to the mixture which will ensure an even spread of cherries throughout the cake.

SERVES 8

welsh cakes

Miss Morgan is a much-loved teacher at Fox who organises our renowned International Evening. She can also be seen dancing down the street at Carnival and manning stalls at the Summer Fair. She is an invaluable member of the Fox community. We loved her Welsh Cakes recipe and then found we'd also been sent Bara Brith, which is similar though more of a bread. We couldn't choose between the two so we kept them both.

225 grams self-raising flour
75 grams caster sugar
75 grams currants
75 grams margarine or butter
1 egg, beaten
Pinch grated nutmeg

1 Rub the margarine into the flour until it is like breadcrumbs.

2 Add the currants, sugar and nutmeg. Mix it all together.

3 Add the beaten egg and mix until it is like dough. You may need a few drops of milk if it's too dry.

4 Roll it out onto a floured board. Cut into scone shapes about 1 centimetre thick.

5 Cook in a heavy frying pan or griddle using a little fat.

6 Cool, sprinkle with sugar and EAT!

MAKES ABOUT 15

speckled bread bara brith

Bara Brith began as any leftover dough from bread making – scattered with dry fruit to preserve. Once cooked, remove from tin, slice thinly and spread with butter. Enjoy with a cup of tea.

250 grams mixed dry fruit

½ litre of tea

125 grams muscovado sugar or soft brown sugar

250 grams self-raising flour

1 large egg

1 Add the sugar to the tea, then add the dried mixed fruit. Soak for about 24 hours.

2 Line a loaf tin with greaseproof paper, and preheat oven to 160°C.

3 Fold in the flour to the mixed fruit, sugar and tea. Add the egg.

4 Cook for 1 hour, test with a skewer to see if cooked – it may need up to 20 minutes more.

MAKES 15 TO 20 SLIM SLICES

puddings

phoenix's gooey chocolate pots

These yummy, gooey chocolate puddings are so easy to make. Honey says they are one of the first puddings her son, Phoenix, learnt to make. Best served hot, they are deliciously rich with a gooey, oozing centre. If serving for pudding, you can prepare and wait until the main course is finished before cooking as they take only 10 minutes. Preheat the oven approximately 30 minutes before you want to cook them. Our lazy tester used the microwave to melt the chocolate and it worked a treat.

125 grams good quality dark chocolate, chopped

125 grams unsalted butter

3 large eggs

150 grams caster sugar

35 grams plain flour

Butter and flour for preparing the ramekins

Whipped or double cream for serving

1 Preheat oven to 200°C.

2 Melt chocolate and butter together, either in microwave or bain-marie.

3 In another bowl whisk together all other ingredients (eggs, sugar and flour).

4 Gradually whisk in melted chocolate and butter and set aside to rest.

5 Butter and flour your four ramekins. Tap to remove excess.

6 Pour mixture into ramekin and put on a baking tray.

7 Place in oven for 10 to 12 minutes or until tops are firm and cracking slightly.

8 Serve with cream. Remember to take care, the ramekins are hot.

SERVES 4

tiramisu

Everybody loves tiramisu! Quite a few of us have sampled Valentina's and it must be one of the best. She told us that we must try to source the real Italian biscuits 'Savoiardi' and make a proper espresso or very strong coffee. The Savoiardi can be found in any Italian delicatessen. They can be replaced with finger biscuits but Valentina refuses to guarantee the result.

4	eggs, separated
120	grams sugar
400	grams mascarpone cheese
400	grams 'Savoiardi' biscuits
½	litre espresso or strong coffee, cooled
30	grams dark cocoa powder

1 Prepare the coffee and let it cool.

2 Mix the yolks with the sugar.

3 Add the mascarpone cheese, mixing until very creamy.

4 Separately whisk the whites until they become very firm.

5 Add the whites to the yolks making sure you mix from bottom to top (this is to make the cream very fluffy).

6 Soak the biscuits, one by one, in the coffee for a few seconds. They should neither soak too much nor too little. Make a layer of biscuits in a small tray.

7 Cover with the cream, then repeat up to 3 or 4 layers.

8 Spread a thick layer of cocoa powder on top.

9 Put in the fridge for at least three hours. Best eaten the next day!

SERVES 8

vanilla poached apricots

This is a recipe Dominique has adapted from a favourite café in Sydney where it is served for breakfast. Don't worry if the apricots go very soft. They should end up with a jammy, sticky consistency. We imagine this is best eaten on a gloriously sunny day overlooking one of Sydney's beaches but failing that, they're awfully cheering under a grey London sky.

250 grams dried apricots

1 tablespoon dark brown sugar

1 vanilla bean pod

600 millilitres water

200 millilitres sheep's milk yoghurt

100 grams almonds, roughly chopped

1 Preheat oven to 170°c.

2 Bring to the boil the water, sugar and vanilla pod (with the pod slit open).

3 Add the apricots then simmer over a low heat for an hour.

4 Spread the almonds on a baking tray and roast in the oven for five minutes.

5 When the almonds have cooled, chop them roughly.

6 Let the apricots cool, and then take out the vanilla pod.

7 Serve the apricots with sheep's milk yoghurt and almonds sprinkled on top.

SERVES 4

rachel's chocolate mousse

Rachel's smile was always there in the playground. And then one day it wasn't. Even those who didn't know her knew her smile. It doesn't sound like enough to say that she is missed. Her husband Stewart copied this recipe out of a small hardback book she kept of all her favourite recipes. It had been transcribed in what he called 'her schoolgirl's handwriting' so it had certainly been used many, many times. Sure, this is a great recipe for kids – Rachel's lovely boys will attest to that. But Rachel also made this for dinner parties (without the chocolate buttons apparently, though we're not sure why). "Like her little black dress," says Stewart, "it dug her out of holes, looked more elaborate than it actually was and always made me happy."

100 grams dark chocolate

2 eggs, separated

150 millilitres double cream

1 packet chocolate buttons (optional – apparently)

1 Melt the chocolate, either in a bowl over a saucepan of boiling water, or slowly in the microwave.

2 Add the melted chocolate to the beaten eggs yolks.

3 Whisk the egg whites.

4 Fold the egg whites gently into the mixture.

5 Divide the light mousse mixture between two bowls and leave in the fridge overnight or until set.

6 Spoon or pipe whipped cream on top of the mousse.

7 Decorate with chocolate buttons or we suppose, raspberries may be a more sophisticated take (if sophistication is what you're after).

SERVES 2

Fox is the proud owner of four happy chickens – Daisy, Ruby, Snowbell and Amy. Each one has its own personality with Snowbell emerging pretty early on as 'top dog' or rather 'top chicken', although Ruby is constantly challenging her for the position. Gloria, our bursar, takes eggsellent care of them. Every morning the chickens are let out of their Eglu coop to roam a safely partitioned section of the playground. They are fed a balanced diet supplemented with food scraps from the kitchen, a plate of which has often been mistaken for Gloria's lunch. This all adds up to very contented chickens and delicious eggs. Generally each chicken lays an egg a day and eggs that are not used are sold in the school office.

the birds, the bees and the fox

Each weekend a rota of local families come in to let the chickens out and make sure they have food and water. Volunteers may keep the eggs they find as a reward. Chicken-carers (as Gloria likes to call them) often bring treats for the chickens like prawn shells, pasta and rocket – at Christmas there may also be the odd mince pie! The chickens are an important part of the Fox community and much loved by all the children – a fact the chicken-carers are only too aware of when taking on their responsibilities each weekend!

The first of Fox's beehives arrived in May 2012 and haven't they settled in nicely! The initial colony of 10,000 Italian bees has grown into a thriving 60,000, so we are already looking to add an additional hive. Our beekeeper is very impressed with our queen who we're told runs an efficient and productive operation (she must be taking inspiration from our other Queen Bee, Gloria). The bee project has already raised so much honey that each child has been able to take home a small sample of their own. Situated as it is near an elderflower bush, the first batch tasted strongly of the elderflower that blossomed in the spring. Later batches have been scented with other flowers in bloom throughout the allotment and the wider community. The bees travel a radius of up to three miles which means they gather pollen from all the surrounding gardens including Kensington Palace and Holland Park. We hope to have jars of Fox honey for sale at the School Fairs and increase the number of hives in the coming years. We are buzzing with excitement over this project! (sorry)

gypsy's white chocolate and raspberry tarts

Holly's daughter Gypsy's signature dish! Delicious and perfect for any occasion, they look pretty and taste wonderful. We can also confirm that they are terrifically easy and quick to prepare. Kids will love making and eating these. They can be stored in an airtight container for three days.

300 grams puff pastry

100 grams white chocolate

2 eggs

100 millilitres double cream

50 grams caster sugar

300 grams raspberries (or strawberries)

Plain flour to sprinkle

Icing sugar to dust

1 Preheat the oven to 180°c.

2 Sprinkle a little flour over a clean surface and turn the dough on to it. Using a rolling pin, gentry roll it until about 2 millimetres thick.

3 Cut the dough into rounds using a pastry cutter or drinking glass and press them into a muffin or cupcake tin.

4 Break up the chocolate into a small heatproof bowl and set the bowl over a saucepan of gently simmering water, making sure that the bottom of the bowl is not touching the water. Stir the chocolate with a wooden spoon until it has melted. Take it off the heat and leave it to cool for a while.

5 Crack the eggs into a large bowl and beat with a balloon whisk until smooth.

6 Whisk in the cream and sugar.

7 Whisk in the melted white chocolate and make sure the mixture is nice and smooth.

8 Carefully fill the tartlet pastry cases with the mixture using a teaspoon.

9 Put the muffin tin into the preheated oven and bake for about 15 minutes, until the pastry is puffy and golden and the filling has risen (it will fall as the tartlets cool).

10 Take the tin out of the oven and leave to cool.

11 Put 3 or 4 raspberries on top of each and dust with icing sugar.

MAKES 12 OR MORE

french crêpes

These are very kid-friendly. Mauve says her family usually has a crêpe feast – savoury crêpes like ham, cheese or mushroom, and then sweet crêpes as dessert when there are leftovers. Most of the time the first crêpe doesn't cook nicely, but don't worry they'll get better! For adults (and kids who like lemon), lemon crêpes are an amazing dessert for dinner parties. Have them ready in advance. Just before serving, heat a pan, drop a tiny bit of butter, put the crêpe in, heat for 30 seconds, turn it over, spread sugar while it is hot, squeeze a little bit of lemon, fold it in half then quarter and it's ready to serve.

3 eggs, beaten

200 grams flour

350 millilitres milk

50 millilitres lager beer (optional but it makes them very light and airy)

1 Put the flour in a bowl, pour the eggs in the centre and mix.

2 Add 50 millilitres milk and mix again.

3 Again 50 millilitres milk and mix well.

4 Then add 50 millilitres beer if you are using it. Mix.

5 Add the remaining milk and mix.

6 Leave to rest for 15 minutes.

7 Oil the pan lightly (and between each crêpe you can use kitchen paper to oil the pan), heat well and start the frying. You can even have a crêpe flipping competition!

MAKES 20 TO 30 CRÊPES

treats

soft almond macaroons

These macaroons were perfected, Saskia says, from a Danish family recipe in order to make various dairy-free/gluten-free friends happy at teatime. They are easy to make with children, who can help mix and roll out the balls, pop them in the paper cases and decorate with almonds or sugar pearls. The macaroons will keep for a week in a tin, and make a good present if you use pretty paper cases. This recipe also works well with other ground nuts – walnuts, pecans, hazelnuts.

250 grams ground almonds

200 grams caster sugar

2 egg whites

1 teaspoon almond or vanilla essence, Di Saronno or Triple Sec liqueur to taste (optional)

Whole almonds, or sugar pearls for decoration

1 Mix ground almonds and sugar together in a bowl.

2 Separate egg whites from yolks. Keep the yolks for another recipe, like Rowley Leigh's strawberry cake. Add egg whites to the sugar and almond mixture. If you are using a flavouring essence or liqueur, add now. Stir with a fork until you have a not too sticky dough.

3 Roll into small balls and pop them in the paper cases. Squash slightly so they are a bit flattened.

4 Decorate with a whole almond, or roll the balls lightly in sugar pearls if you like.

5 Put in a hot oven for ten minutes. They should be lightly browned and firm, crisp on the outside but still soft and moist inside.

MAKES A DOZEN

top secret pancakes

Giselle's grandfather only ever let his grandchildren call him Luis. Every Sunday he made pancakes for them and each time he told the same story. The story was that a tiny Chinaman called Dr. Fu-Manchu (lifted from the 1920's series) was after Luis's famous pancake recipe. To protect it, the children had to close all the doors and cover the keyholes (since he was small enough to get through). They would all stand guard by the doors while Luis cooked. Her favourite part was when he made animal shapes out of the tiny drippings of batter when it was nearly finished. Luis sounds like someone we'd like share a pancake or two with.

45 grams butter

225 grams plain flour

¼ teaspoon salt

2 teaspoons caster sugar

1 teaspoon baking powder

½ teaspoon bicarbonate of soda

1 egg

300 millilitres buttermilk

100 millilitres whole milk

1 Check that the doors are manned and the keyholes are covered to protect Luis's recipe.

2 Melt the butter and leave to cool slightly. Put the oven on low to keep the pancakes warm as they are cooked.

3 Put the flour, salt, sugar, baking powder and bicarbonate soda into a bowl.

4 Put the egg, buttermilk and milk into a smaller bowl or jug and give it a whisk, then stir in the melted butter.

5 Now add the wet ingredients to the dry and stir just enough to combine. Don't over mix or the pancakes will become chewy. This really does make a difference.

6 Double check that keyholes are covered.

7 Put a heavy-based frying pan on a medium heat and brush the base with melted butter. Use a large spoon to dollop pancakes into the pan (you'll probably need to do this in at least 2 batches) and cook until they begin to look dry and bubbly on top: depending on the heat of your pan, this should take about 3 minutes. Flip over and cook for another couple of minutes until golden. Put into the oven to keep warm while you cook the remaining pancakes, unless you have customers ready and waiting.

8 Serve with your choice of butter, maple syrup or bacon. Or, of course, all three.

MAKES 10 PANCAKES

dulce de leche milk caramel

Dulce de Leche originated in Argentina in 1829, in Cañuelasi, Buenos Aires, when a servant preparing 'La lechada' (a combination of milk and sugar) left it on the heat when she thought an enemy attack was underway. You can eat this in so many ways: on its own, on bread, with croissants, with crêpes, you can use it as filling for a sponge cake, or with ice cream (this is how Barbara's girls love it). When Barbara's mother visits from Argentina, the first thing they do, when the suitcases have been put away, is start a saucepan of it bubbling on the hob. As three generations sit down to catch up, they take turns stirring the luscious liquid as it thickens.

3 litres whole fat milk

800 grams sugar

1 teaspoon vanilla essence

½ teaspoon bicarbonate of soda

1 Heat the milk.

2 Before the milk boils, add the sugar, vanilla and bicarbonate of soda.

3 Boil at a high heat and mix with a wooden spoon for 2½ hours.

4 It's ready when it has a brownish colour and starts shaping into a more solid consistency. Take a little bit of 'dulce' with a spoon, put it in a plate and let it cool down. At this point you can see the consistency.

5 Once ready, take it off the heat and let it cool down.

Note: Once it cools down, it should be refrigerated. Consume within a month.

MAKES ABOUT TWO JARS

fox says, "eat your fruit!"

It's no accident that we've placed an exhortation to eat your fruit in amongst a groaning 'Desserts' section. We did start off trying to promote healthy eating with the Fox Pot but everyone kept sending us puddings! Luckily lots of people also shared with us the different ways they eat fruit in their country and we were amazed at all the variations.

oranges

In Sicily there is a tradition of preparing a salad with oranges and fennel. We've also come across a delicious combination of oranges and smoked fish.

strawberries

Strawberries and cream is always a hands-down favourite at the Summer Fair, but why not try these variations?

Jerry's mother says that in Hungary, she grew up eating strawberries with powdered sugar and his grandfather cannot imagine eating strawberries any other way even now.

Rueben's mother, Rachel, prepares strawberries with freshly ground black pepper.

Harper's grandma marinates them in balsamic vinegar, divine.

apples and pears

In France, everyone eats cheese with slices of apple and pears – and that tradition has spread widely.

In Italy, it's cheese with pears and the old saying "Al contadino non far sapere quanto è buono il cacio con le pere" (Don't let the farmer know how good cheese is with pears). It comes highly recommended by student Matteo.

In Yorkshire, they've put their own special twist on it – Ben's grandfather always insists on having apple pie and cheddar cheese (and cheddar cheese with fruitcake too!).

pomegranate

The pomegranate has always held great significance in ancient civilizations and has been hailed as having innumerable healing powers. All over the Middle East and Central Asia, pomegranate is used as a garnish on all kinds of dishes and pomegranate molasses is used in various savory recipes.

In Azerbaijan, Andrey's mother tell us that pomegranate is served with sugar. In Lebanon, they go a step further and add a few teaspoons of orange blossom water. Iskander's mother grew up eating this and the fragrance is a strong reminder of the end of long hot summers.

melon

In Italy, we have the eternal classic of Parma ham with melon.

In the Middle East and Central Asia, there is a different take on fruit and cheese. In Lebanon, Iskander's jedo (grandfather in Arabic) grew up eating fresh watermelon with cubes or slices of haloumi cheese. Substitute haloumi with feta cheese and you could be in Azerbaijan.

pineapple

Why stop at apples or pears and cheese? How about that English 70's party food classic of cheese and pineapple on a stick! Mundane we know – but still great as well as delicious!

In Singapore and Southern China, pineapple is made even more zesty when dipped in soy sauce.

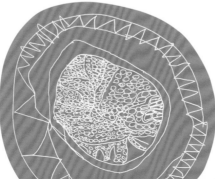

jodie terry | **australia**

anzac biscuits

When Jodie was little she remembers there always being a tin full of these at her grandmother's house. Those were the best Anzac biscuits – chewy and crunchy at the same time. There are many stories about how the Anzac biscuit came to be; the most common being that they were made to send to the ANZAC troops in World War One. They're great for kids to make as they are hard to mess up. Now that Jodie makes her own, she lets Eva, Joy and May mix the ingredients with their hands and then make the balls for putting on the tray (although strangely, she says, quite a bit of the mixture gets lost between bowl and tray…)

100	grams coconut
150	grams flour
100	grams rolled oats
150	grams brown sugar
125	grams butter
2	tablespoons golden syrup
1	teaspoon bicarbonate of soda

1 Preheat oven to 160°C.

2 Line a baking tray with greaseproof paper.

3 Combine oats, flour, coconut and brown sugar.

4 Melt butter with golden syrup.

5 Dissolve bicarbonate of soda with boiling water then stir into melted butter mixture.

6 Pour the foaming butter mixture into the flour mixture and stir well.

7 Roll level tablespoons of the mixture into balls and place on a tray 5 centimetres apart.

8 Press down lightly with fork to flatten and bake for 10 minutes.

9 Allow to cool slightly on tray before transferring to wire rack.

MAKES 20 BISCUITS

moose muffins

Fox mother Jenny says that unlike the sugary cupcakes you tend to get here in the UK, Canadian muffins are traditionally healthy, but also delicious. Her boys, Jeremy and Toby, have made this recipe with her many times. They are in charge of putting the liners in the tin, mixing wet and dry ingredients and of course eating any wayward chocolate chips! The flaxseed adds a tasty nuttiness to the muffins and like all the other ingredients you can pick it up at Whole Foods Market. These make the perfect after school treat.

250	grams whole wheat flour
250	grams all purpose four
175	grams ground flaxseed
50	grams semi sweet chocolate chips or diced dried fruit
1	teaspoon baking powder
1	teaspoon bicarbonate of soda
1	teaspoon cinnamon
½	teaspoon salt
3	very ripe mashed bananas
175	millilitres Canadian (of course) maple syrup
175	millilitres buttermilk or ½ cup sunflower oil if you prefer dairy free
2	free range eggs

1 Preheat oven to 200°c.

2 Place paper liners into muffin tin.

3 Mix dry ingredients.

4 In separate bowl, mix wet ingredients.

5 Combine wet and dry ingredients until just combined.

6 Put into 10 to 12 muffin cups. Bake for 20 to 25 minutes (or until an inserted toothpick comes out clean). Mmmmuffins!

SERVES 10 TO 12

tablet fudge

Rachel is one of our Mums who was once a Fox pupil herself. Three of her children have attended Fox and we dread the day when we will say goodbye to her. She makes such a fantastic contribution to our school. Maybe she'll be back one day as a granny? This is a Scottish recipe passed on to her by her "beautiful and lovely friend," Kate Wickham. They used to make it for the Fox School Fair surrounded by their babies Hamish, Dylan, Emily, Isobel, Perdy, Isla and Reuben. They wrapped it in small brown greaseproof paper tied with a tartan ribbon. It's the perfect Christmas gift for your child to make.

200 millilitres milk

1 large tin condensed milk

900 grams sugar

100 grams butter

1 Melt the butter and sugar.

2 Add the condensed milk and the teacup of milk.

3 Stir and turn up the heat and keep stirring until it reaches boiling point. Turn the heat down low and stir for 45 minutes.

4 Other suggestions are to add, as an optional ingredient, either: cinnamon, coconut, fig, ginger, lemon, orange, peppermint, vanilla, walnut, chocolate or pure vanilla essence to the tablet recipe.

5 Remove from the heat and beat 60 times with a wooden spoon. Put a little bit on a plate and if it sets then it's ready to be put onto the shallow trays.

6 Score the tablet's surface in squares and allow to set.

SERVES…THAT DEPENDS!

butter shortbread

When Ailsa's family want shortbread this is the recipe they turn to. It's taken from an old Scottish cookbook that was passed down by Ailsa's grandmother from the West Coast of Scotland. It actually belonged to her mother before her. Ailsa prefers to cut the shortbread into hearts or stars rather than the traditional petticoat shape. The buttery sweetness cries out for a nice cold glass of milk to accompany it, or since we're coming to the end of the book, perhaps a wee dram. Use non-stick baking parchment to line the baking sheet.

110 grams butter
 55 grams caster sugar
110 grams plain flour
 55 grams rice flour

1 Cream sugar and butter until pale and fluffy.

2 Sift the flours and work into a smooth paste.

3 Roll out thinly on a floured worktop.

4 Cut out shapes with cutters.

5 Bake on a greased sheet at 170°c for 15 minutes.

SERVES 8

chocolate, banana and avocado shake

This is Will's other sneaky 'how to get greens into your kids' recipe (his other is crispy seaweed in the 'Sides'). He'd like to take the credit for this one but can't. He and his wife, Sam, happened upon it in Bali, watching the football in a bar with the kids. "Getting the colour green into your kids isn't easy but this recipe manages to do it by using lots of avocados and bananas, hiding behind a small flurry of drinking chocolate," says Will. "The chocolate powder has sugar in it but not enough to outweigh the goodness of the avocado." Ollie Millet, Fox's PE teacher, is always telling the kids to drink smoothies for energy – he'd certainly approve of this recipe.

1 avocado

2 bananas

2 teaspoons Cadbury's drinking chocolate

200 millilitres milk (or to your taste)

1 Put all ingredients in a blender. If the bananas and avocados are nice and ripe this should only take about ten seconds. Yum.

MAKES 2 SMOOTHIES

hot spiced cider

For Kezia's family this is the smell of Christmas. Her grandmother and mother (who taught at Fox when she arrived in London from New York in 1966) had a large pot on the stove throughout the holidays that they would replenish daily. Kezia is now a mother at Fox and she continues the tradition. This spiced apple cider is now sold alongside Mulled Wine at the Fox Winter Fair. The recipe below is how the Pierce/Summerfield family like it but feel free to adjust the spice levels to your own liking and create your own family's spiced apple recipe. If preferred you can replace the various spices with a ¼ teaspoon of mixed spice.

1	litre apple juice
1	tablespoon dark brown sugar
½	teaspoon ground cinnamon
¼	teaspoon ground allspice
1	pinch ground cloves
1	pinch ground ginger
1	pinch ground nutmeg
1	stick cinnamon
1	orange studded with whole cloves

1 Mix apple juice and brown sugar in a pot and heat on a medium heat.

2 Add spices and continue to heat until piping hot but not boiling.

3 For best results allow to cool and reheat to just under a boil

4 Add the cinnamon stick and studded orange.

5 Allow to infuse for a while before serving.

SERVES 10

INDEX

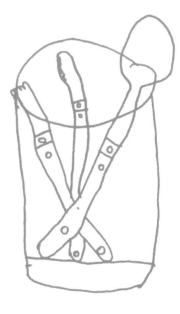

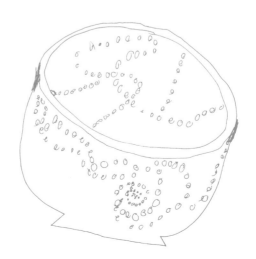

ACKNOWLEDGEMENTS

The Fox Pot team would like to thank everyone who contributed to this project, in particular Elif Aykas who started it all; Chai Kang for her recipe roundup; Holly Ross for being the woman to make things happen; Amanda Bannister for keeping us ship shape and above board; Eddie Batha and Mariela Manso for the extra design hands; Sheila Rea Garrett for getting it off the paper and into the computer and Dominique Jackson and Brian Terry, for their eagle-eyes.

Thanks to everyone who cooked food for us: Shaun Acharya, Che Ya Ahmed, Saskia Baron, Sandra Crane, Susan Deliss, Hazel Foo, Angela Hammes, Dominique Jackson, Chai Kang, Danny Lidgate, Sheila Rea Garrett, Shy Robson, George Venieris, Joy Wu, Valerie Yeang, Zuraiha Zainull Rashid.

We owe a debt of gratitude to the people in our community who have supported us, in particular the chefs and restaurateurs who were so generous with the recipes that are their livelihood. Elisabeth Luard in particular provided us with her invaluable insight and experience, not to mention a delicious recipe.

The following chefs have very kindly donated recipes for this book: Sally Clarke; Gennaro Contaldo; John Devitt; Daniel and Hazel Foo; Bill Granger; Rowley Leigh; Lidgate Butchers; Elisabeth Luard; Jamie Oliver; Yotam Ottolenghi; Nina Rich; George Venieris; Valentine Warner; Whole Foods Market.

We are grateful to Kensington Library for its help with the history of Fox and to Jenny Wedgbury from Kensington Palace, its conservators and the Royal Collection.

Thank you to Siobhan Ferguson Photography for her beautiful photos of Notting Hill.

A special thanks to Charles Adamah, Ben McMullin and Amir Sheik for their support beyond the call of duty; Head Teacher Paul Cotter for his enthusiasm for the project; and, as ever, the amazing Gloria Double and Serena Lott-Lavigna. All the beautiful artwork displayed here is the work of Fox children of all ages. Thank you for bringing your individual talents to the pages of this book. We would like to thank Fox art teacher Sarah Edwards for working tirelessly with the children.

Finally, thanks to the parents, staff and children of Fox whose contributions have made this book and whose hearts and souls make our school.

PHOTOGRAPHY

Article on page 153, "The winner of our raffle for bath oil and soap is...The Queen!" by Duncan Larcombe reproduced, with permission, from The Sun 17/09/2007, © The Sun, 17/09/2007

Cover photograph and other photography by Siobhan Ferguson.

Jamie Oliver "Summer Frittata" on page 110 © Matt Russell Recipe © Jamie Oliver www.jamieoliver.com

"Lidgate Diamond Jubilee Pie" on page 105 was photographed on 17 May 2012 at Kensington Palace in the King's Gallery

REFERENCES

Survey of London XXXVII North Kensington 1973

Charles James Fox, L.G. Mitchell, Oxford University Press 1992

Holland House, Leslie Mitchell, Duckworth 1980

The Home of the Hollands 1605 – 1900, John Murray, Albermarle St W1

Chronicles of Holland House 1820 – 1900, John Murray, Albermarle St W1

Jodie Terry Head Writer and Editor

Giselle Cuello Landers Book and cover design, food and other photography

Jenny Hewlett Project Manager, marketing and distribution

François Kojey-Strauss Food styling, testing and photography, copy editing, writing

Alison Cooper Writing and editing, marketing and distribution

Tammy Boutel Writing and project management

Poppy Luard Lee Copy editing, food styling

Shy Robson Marketing

Christina Bartholomew Writing and editing

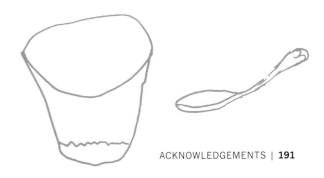

Pesta